With Thine Own Eyes

WITH THINE OWN EYES

Why Imitate the Past
When We Can Investigate Reality?

by

Ronald Tomanio, Diane Iverson and Phyllis Ring

George Ronald
Oxford

George Ronald, *Publisher*
Oxford
www.grbooks.com

*A catalogue record for this book is available
from the British Library*

ISBN 978–0–85398–578–5

Cover design: Steiner Graphics

O Son of Spirit!

The best beloved of all things in My sight is Justice; turn not away therefrom if thou desirest Me, and neglect it not that I may confide in thee. By its aid thou shalt see with thine own eyes and not through the eyes of others, and shalt know of thine own knowledge and not through the knowledge of thy neighbour. Ponder this in thy heart; how it behoveth thee to be. Verily justice is My gift to thee and the sign of My loving-kindness. Set it then before thine eyes.

Bahá'u'lláh[1]

CONTENTS

ACKNOWLEDGEMENTS

The authors dedicate this book with their gratitude to and for the institution and presence of the Universal House of Justice in the world.

Ron Tomanio dedicates it to his mother, Dr Mary E. Tomanio, DC; his father, Samuel Tomanio; his brother, Richard Tomanio; his beloved wife, Karen Tomanio; and their daughters, Laurel and Julia Tomanio. He also wishes to acknowledge George Ronald, Publisher, Justice St Rain and One Voice Press for the encouragement each has provided.

Diane dedicates this book to her parents, Elsie Grace Williams Iverson and Joseph Carl Iverson, whose spirits and example helped lead her to Bahá'u'lláh, and to the thousands of souls she's been privileged to meet who have enriched her life and helped provide the polishing she needed, and innumerable angels who have provided emotional, practical, material and spiritual sustenance. She also wishes to acknowledge her brother, James L. Iverson of Madison, Wisconsin; his wife, Sally; and daughters, Kari and Ellen and grandson, Kyle, for remembering, always; Sandra Clark for a constant, balanced perspective; and Jack Leonard, Larry Akeley and Randy Boyd for unique friendship, support and encouragement in this work.

Phyllis dedicates this book to the memory of Marian and Ted Lippitt, Terry Jane Cassiday and Laura Howland. She also wishes to honour and thank her husband, Jonathan S. Ring, for his insight, his tenderness, his playful humour and the abiding gift of his spiritual companionship day by day.

The material in this book was developed through interaction with many others who attended workshops and classes that the authors facilitated at conferences, summer schools and in private homes. All these participants are, in one sense, our co-authors and we thank them for their contributions and enthusiastic interest.

We must also acknowledge Alden Kent, who helped present aspects of this material with us for many years; Dr Charlotte Gallagher who supported our classes and wrote the Preface; Jon Ring and J. Michael Kafes, who supported classes and encouraged us to persevere; and Doug McAdam, our living grandfather in this work. We all express our thanks to Justice St Rain for giving valuable advice on an earlier version of the manuscript.

We extend special gratitude to our spiritual ancestors in this effort on whose shoulders we stand, without whom this book would not be possible and from whom we received invaluable seen and unseen assistance: in particular we thank Mírzá Abu'l-Faḍl, Sarah Jane Farmer, Henrietta Emogene Martin Hoagg, Marian Crist Lippitt, Dr Daniel C. Jordan, Henry and Sissy Weil, Elizabeth Thomas, Leonard Hippchen and many more than we can currently know.

PREFACE

The authors have been reflecting for more than 15 years on how to define the steps of spiritual transformation from the perspective of the Bahá'í Faith. They have discovered that it is a process of advancement and retreat, of seeing clearly with our spiritual eyes and then not being able to see at all when ego takes over and directs us towards a materialistic focus on survival. I met a woman a few weeks ago who said that she had spent a great deal of her life not believing in God. During a difficult time she had an epiphany in which she believed God spoke to her and told her that her mission in life was to 'learn, grow and love'.

Perhaps all of us have this mission but if we don't have an understanding as to how this can happen, the journey can involve endless steps that lead nowhere. This wonderfully practical and human book invites us to turn our attention towards investigating spiritual reality, describes how that experience is met and encountered and why it is indescribably fulfilling – the very purpose for which we were created.

We find that the first step in this process is to understand the single condition for us on this plane of existence: service in surrender to truth, within the Covenant that God has renewed with humanity from age to age. As they explore the process – and pitfalls – that we can encounter in this investigation of reality, the authors make use of two questions to bring the above concept into sharper focus:

1) At this moment in time, what is the act of service I am capable of giving that the other person is capable of receiving?

2) At this moment in time, what is the act of service I am capable of receiving that the other person is capable of giving?

The authors encourage reflection on many of our behaviours, some relevant and some not relevant, in our quest for spiritual transformation. They describe how, as we pursue this path, our ego or 'insistent self', the 'mind we've made up', sets up one potential roadblock after another as it draws from blind imitation of the past, as well as such old habits as a conditioned tendency towards fighting evil rather than creating solutions. Some of the steps identified here that can guide the soul safely along the road of development include: understanding our need to choose with our free will acts of service commensurate with our spiritual understanding; listening carefully to our intuitive voice; knowing our purpose; facing and regarding our fears as illusory; and acquiring a sin-covering eye.

Using the Bahá'í writings, the authors engage us in an ever-deepening understanding of the soul, of inner vision and of the spirit of faith. They assert that as the soul, using free will choice, is able to offer and receive acts of service under the Covenant of God that Bahá'u'lláh has renewed in this age, the spirit of faith grows within us and helps establish a self-sustaining cycle of spiritual transformation. This transformative process, which begins first in our mind's eye, quickly moves to our hearts and, like the stones being washed in a swiftly moving stream, wears away doubt and fear and replaces them with certitude – the certitude found in surrendering to truth, which allows us to 'hear with different ears and see with different eyes' and to experience the peace and happiness that are always abiding within our very truest selves.

The Bahá'í writings that abound throughout the text serve as a magnet drawing readers from that uncomfortable place of crisis where one recognizes one's behaviour as woefully far from the Truth to one of hope that with continued resolve the soul can find its true liberation as it comes to embody its true purpose.

The book is composed of short sections on specific topics, each with a sequential, distilled concept that can be pondered by itself or be utilized as a building block towards the next concept. This then allows readers the possibility of growth within an individualized time frame. All of these factors combine to make this an excellent study guide for individuals or groups of people. Many of these concepts have been tested in a classroom setting and those who have taken the classes have broadened their spiritual horizons.

The authors also suggest that investigating how to live from one's spiritual reality, beyond being a priceless gift in itself, allows an even more vital opportunity: to be a means by which a divinely designed healing medicine can reach and transform the ills and suffering that afflict our world.

Spiritual transformation's ultimate goal, the authors assert, is to create unconditionally loving relationships and communities in order that the potentialities latent within them may be manifested in this Day of God. Every educational system, beginning with those involved with the needs of the youngest children and embracing all, up through the oldest and wisest adults, would benefit from learning and practising the steps of spiritual investigation described here. All the helping communities – psychologists, social workers, doctors, nurses and more – would have patients and clients with fewer maladies and troubles if they were taught such steps of spiritual realization and encouraged to use them on a daily basis. In addition, 'foe' would become friend, disillusionment would change to wonder and doubt could evolve to trust.

To conclude, the following poem, 'Autobiography in Five Short Chapters' from the book *There's a Hole in My Sidewalk* by Portia Nelson, seems apropos:

I

I walk down the street.
There is a deep hole in the sidewalk.
I fall in
I am lost . . . I am helpless
It isn't my fault.
It takes me forever to find a way out.

II

I walk down the same street.
There is a deep hole in the sidewalk.
I pretend I don't see it.
I fall in again.
I can't believe I am in the same place.
but, it isn't my fault.
It still takes a long time to get out.

III
I walk down the same street.
There is a deep hole in the sidewalk.
I see it is there.
I still fall in . . . it's a habit.
My eyes are open.
I know where I am.
It is my fault.
I get out immediately.

IV
I walk down the same street.
There is a deep hole in the sidewalk
I walk around it.

V
I walk down another street.

If we truly want to get out of the hole in which many of us may find ourselves, the companionship of this highly informative and infinitely accessible guide to investigation of spiritual reality will not only warm our hearts but inspire and challenge us to action.

Charlotte Gallagher, PhD

THE PURPOSE OF THIS BOOK

The holy Manifestations of God come into the world to dispel the darkness of the animal, or physical, nature of man, to purify him from his imperfections in order that his heavenly and **spiritual nature** may become quickened, his divine qualities awakened, his perfections visible, his potential powers revealed and **all the virtues of the world of humanity latent within him may come to life**.[2]

Only our spiritual nature can look beyond outward appearances, first impressions and personality flaws to see 'all the virtues of the world of humanity latent within' ourselves and each other.

In its 2008 message to Bahá'ís throughout the world, the Faith's international governing body, the Universal House of Justice, called upon Bahá'ís everywhere to 'perceive honour and nobility in every human being'.[3]

This phrase serves to banish any remaining fear we may have in our hearts that we do not have access to this lofty reality. It is a gentle reminder that when Bahá'u'lláh affirmed, 'Noble have I created thee,'[4] He was speaking to us. Not some of us. Not most of us. Not everyone except me – but all of us.

We don't pretend to be able to inform others of the nature of their own individual realities – who they are and what their purpose is. We provide relevant quotations from the Bahá'í writings, but each of us is the only person capable of investigating and discovering our unique identity and purpose. How 'honour and nobility' manifest themselves in us – each a unique creation of God – is a one-of-a-kind and wondrous journey. That is not our opinion but an unambiguous statement made by 'Abdu'l-Bahá, included in an upcoming chapter.

What we are attempting to offer here are some practical tools inspired by the life of 'Abdu'l-Bahá, who offered a living example of a life of true service as He sought to bring the healing message of His father, Bahá'u'lláh, to humanity. Also included here is guidance from the sacred writings which, when applied on a daily basis, slowly but surely results in the spiritual nature becoming the decision-maker in our lives.

In recent years news media repeatedly report that more than half of the people in the United States, as well as others in many parts of the world, have made changes while on their spiritual path, indicating that there is a widespread yearning to know the answers to the questions of who we are and why we are here.

Such questions, which this book attempts to address, are ones critical to the very survival of a desperate humanity. Yet humanity is also being invited towards a prospect far, far beyond mere survival, a glorious, unprecedented age of fulfilment that has been spoken of in the prophecies of all faiths.

This, the Bahá'í writings affirm, is exactly why the Manifestations of God, those bestowers of humanity's spiritual teachings, have come into the world. Yet where is the transformation that they promised would manifest itself in humanity? When and how will that 'honour and nobility' spoken of by the Universal House of Justice become manifest in the world and 'all the virtues of the world of humanity' latent within each and every soul come to life?

Perhaps the real, underlying questions are: What is our individual part in this great promise? How have we been invited to participate in it? What is our own will and willingness? What will our own response be?

The process of fully addressing such questions, the authors suggest, the power for which was released into creation more than 150 years ago, brings us into contact with our own highest reality. It involves coming to understand who it is that we are created to be. This inevitably leads to new ways of seeing ourselves, each other and our world. And equally inevitably, it welcomes into being a whole new way of thinking that evolves out of love and attraction towards those latent spiritual gifts waiting to be revealed, rather than continuing to perpetuate the near-instinctual reactions that arise from fear rooted in preoccupation with physical survival. That crippling fear has kept humanity, human thinking and our greatest possibilities entrapped for aeons but in this new and truly wondrous age there's a door that's been opened wider than heaven and earth through which we've been invited to pass. Are we ready to embrace the truth that our own truest and deepest reality, that for which we were created, is a presence and power in whose light fear and the trappings of mere survival disappear like shadows?

As this book passes from its authors' hands after years of shaping its content in workshops and other collaborative-learning settings, our sincerest hope is that every reader may come to know the joy, freedom and fulfilment that accompany every conscious effort, as 'Abdu'l-Bahá so repeatedly urged, to investigate our reality.

THE ROOTS OF SUFFERING

A Letter of the Universal House of Justice, 19 November 1974

The letter of the Universal House of Justice set out below is referred to as 'Comments on the Bahá'í Attitude Toward Material Suffering'. When we decided to write a book about the process of investigating our individual reality, the question arose as to whether there might be a possible sequence that such an investigation would follow.

We found that the following letter, and its highlighted paragraph in particular, describes quite specifically in sequential order what we 'desperately need to know'.

19 November 1974

To: The National Spiritual Assembly of the Bahá'ís of Italy

Dear Bahá'í friends,

In your letter of 11 September you say that the questions of how to help the Third World or the poor who are suffering under calamities are much discussed in your community and you wish to know whether to create a special fund for such needs, to ask for special contributions from time to time, or whether there are other ways in which you could help.

It is understandable that Bahá'ís who witness the miserable conditions under which so many human beings have to live, or who hear of a sudden disaster that has struck a certain area of the world, are moved to do something practical to ameliorate those conditions and to help their suffering fellow-mortals.

There are many ways in which help can be rendered. Every Bahá'í has the duty to acquire a trade or profession through which he will earn that wherewith he can support himself and his family; in the choice of such work he can seek those activities which are of benefit to his fellowmen and not merely those which promote his personal interests, still less those whose effects are actually harmful.

There are also the situations in which an individual Bahá'í or a Spiritual Assembly is confronted with an urgent need which neither justice nor compassion could allow to go unheeded and unhelped. How many are the stories told of 'Abdu'l-Bahá in such situations, when He would even take off a garment He was wearing and give it to a shivering man in rags.

But in our concern for such immediate obvious calls upon our succour we must not allow ourselves to forget the continuing, appalling burden of suffering under which millions of human beings are always groaning – a burden which they have borne for century upon century and which it is the mission of Bahá'u'lláh to lift at last. The principal cause of this suffering, which one can witness wherever one turns, is the corruption of human morals and the prevalence of prejudice, suspicion, hatred, untrustworthiness, selfishness and tyranny among men. **It is not merely material well-being that people need. What they desperately need is to know how to live their lives – they need to know who they are, to what purpose they exist, and how they should act towards one another; and, once they know the answers to these questions they need to be helped to gradually apply these answers to everyday behaviour.** It is to the solution of this basic problem of mankind that the greater part of all our energy and resources should be directed. There are mighty agencies in this world, governments, foundations, institutions of many kinds with tremendous financial resources which are working to improve the material lot of human beings. Anything we Bahá'ís could add to such resources in the way of special funds or contributions would be a negligible drop in the ocean. However, alone among men we have the divinely given remedy for the real ills of mankind; no one else is doing or can do this most important work, and if we divert our energy and our funds into fields in which others are already doing more than we can hope to do, we shall be delaying the diffusion of the Divine Message which is the most important task of all.

Because of such an attitude, and also because of our refusal to become involved in politics, Bahá'ís are often accused of holding aloof from the 'real problems' of their fellowmen. But when we hear this accusation let us not forget that those who make it are usually idealistic materialists to whom material good is the only 'real' good, whereas we know that the working of the material world is merely a reflection of spiritual conditions and until the spiritual conditions can be changed there can be no lasting change for the better in material affairs.

We should also remember that most people have no clear concept of the sort of world they wish to build, nor how to go about building it. Even those who are concerned to improve conditions are therefore reduced to combatting every apparent evil that takes their attention. Willingness to fight against evils, whether in the form of conditions or embodied in evil men, has thus become for most people the touchstone by which they judge a person's moral worth. Bahá'ís, on the other hand, know the goal they are working towards and know what they must do, step by step, to attain it. **Their whole energy is directed towards the building of the good, a good which has such a positive strength that in the face of it the multitude of evils – which are in essence negative – will fade away and be no more. To enter into the quixotic tournament of demolishing one by one the evils in the world is, to a Bahá'í, a vain waste of time and effort.** His whole life is directed towards proclaiming the Message of Bahá'u'lláh, reviving the spiritual life of his fellowmen, uniting them in a divinely created World Order, and then, as the Order grows in strength and influence, he will see the power of that Message transforming the whole human society and progressively solving the problems and removing the injustices which have so long bedevilled the world.

With loving Bahá'í greetings,
The Universal House of Justice[5]

Within this letter the Universal House of Justice has laid out a sequence of what the people of the world – each and every human soul – desperately need to know:

1) Who they are

2) To what purpose they exist

3) How they should act towards one another

4) And, once they know the answers to these questions they need to be helped to gradually apply these answers to **everyday behaviour.**

It is instructive to note that the fourth step tells us that it is only *after* we come to know our identity and purpose and follow a code of behaviour revealed by the Manifestation of God that we are in a position to know how we should act towards one another and are ready to form healthy relationships.

Any significant journey requires a map describing how to get from where we are to our desired destination. This letter is the road map that the chapters of this book will attempt to follow, addressing each of the questions posed by the Universal House of Justice in the same sequence as that in which they are listed in the letter. First, however, the book will address what 'Abdu'l-Bahá repeatedly described as major obstacles to beginning such a journey of personal investigation.

A discussion about the need to abandon the illusion that there is moral worth in fighting evil and instead to direct all our energies towards the building of the good can be found primarily in chapter 1.

SECTION ONE

As we have read and reread the extraordinary letter of 19 November 1974 from the Universal House of Justice, we have been left with one big question: Why, after thousands of years of heart-rending sacrifices by numerous Prophets and their devoted followers, has humanity arrived at the point of profound ignorance – ignorance to such an extent that the supreme institution of the Bahá'í Faith has said in unequivocal language that **we don't know who we are, what our purpose is or how we should behave towards one another?** The very word 'ignorance' implies that something is being ignored or overlooked, does it not? And, it seems, we are being called to investigate and discover what that is.

That big question led to another inevitable question: Have the efforts of these great teachers and their followers been in vain?

While we believe that the answer to this second question is a resounding 'No', we have also reached the conclusion that it is impossible to answer these questions to their fullest extent unless the power to investigate reality, and the experience of it, rests firmly in the hands of the individual, and that such ultimate empowerment was revealed to humanity only quite recently in its history.

When He came to the West late in His life, after decades of imprisonment because of the revolutionary teachings that His father, Bahá'u'lláh, had brought to liberate the human soul in this day, 'Abdu'l-Bahá told His listeners:

> First among the great principles revealed by Him is that of the investigation of reality . . . The announcement of this principle is not found in any of the sacred Books of the past.[1]

Until Bahá'u'lláh's advent as a Prophet and Manifestation of God in

1863, it was the governmental and religious rulers who had taken charge of the investigation of reality for the largely illiterate masses of people. Although some progress was made, civilizations had inevitably degenerated because the people blindly imitated the model given to them by these same rulers, and the codes imposed upon them, especially as those rulers and leaders sought personal power. Bahá'u'lláh's declaration that it was now the Creator's Will that all investigate reality for themselves and that the circumstances of life would evolve and advance so that this would be possible was both unprecedented and a major challenge to those who sought to hold worldly power.

The next two chapters examine two fundamental stumbling blocks to that investigation of reality to which Bahá'u'lláh has called and invited us.

FIGHTING EVIL

'A Vain Waste of Time and Effort'

If people only realized it, the inner life of the spirit is that which counts, but they are so blinded by desires and so misled that they have brought upon themselves all the suffering we see at present in the world. The Bahá'ís seek to lead people back to a knowledge of their true selves and the purpose for which they were created, and thus to their greatest happiness and highest good.[2]

The letter of the Universal House of Justice of 19 November 1974 on material suffering contains two major themes. The first links the behaviour that fosters material suffering to a profound overall ignorance of the fundamental reality of each individual's true identity and purpose. In reflecting on this theme together with what is emphasized in this chapter's opening quotation, it seems clear that the greatest well-being of the individual, the family and society are all inextricably linked to a knowledge and understanding of our true, spiritual identity and the purpose for which we have been created.

The 1974 letter's second theme explains that humankind's lack of a clear vision of an ideal world – no vision of the 'good' – has left it with no apparent option but to focus all its energy on 'combatting every apparent evil' in the hope that if all the evils could be destroyed, a better world would somehow emerge. The letter describes such an attempt as a 'vain waste of time and effort'.

It is interesting to note also that in His teachings, all of which revolve around the oneness of humankind, Bahá'u'lláh categorically forbids contention of any kind. If we would investigate reality and seek a building of the good, it also seems clear that 'fighting evil', whether without or within, is not only a 'vain waste of time and effort' but counterproductive.

As it combines these two themes in the letter, the Universal House of Justice is inviting us instead to travel the positive (i.e. real) path that the 'building of the good' represents. And, we would suggest, a 'building of the good' – that which is real and lasting – can best begin when the part of us that is real and lasting, our soul, becomes aware of its true identity and purpose.

Think in terms of constructing a building, whether a simple cottage or a tall skyscraper. No matter what is being built, the foundation must be rock-solid or the structure will collapse. Perhaps it will not happen right away but the building will inevitably come crashing down.

Likewise, material good that does not have a spiritual foundation will prove to be a house of cards that sooner or later will fall apart.

When a sufficient number of individuals in a society successfully answer the questions of 'who they are' and 'to what purpose they exist', the quality of 'everyday behaviour' improves dramatically and material suffering gradually abates. The Universal House of Justice goes a giant step further by stating that it is not just material suffering that will disappear but that a 'multitude of evils . . . will fade away and be no more'.

The implications of this historic letter are far-reaching and affect every aspect of world civilization. However, this book is focused on the individual. Thus the questions before each of us are:

- Do I have a clear vision of who I truly am?

- Am I 'building the good' in my life or indulging in 'a vain waste of time and effort' trying to fight the evil or imperfections that I see within me and around me?

Notice the inclusion of the word 'vain', implying that it is a waste of time and brings no useful result.

What happens when an individual uses 'the willingness to fight against evils' to 'judge a person's moral worth'?

To answer that question, it helps to have a definition of evil. When asked, 'What is evil?' 'Abdu'l-Bahá replied:

Evil is imperfection. Sin is the state of man in the world of the baser nature, for in nature exist defects such as injustice, tyranny, hatred, hostility, strife: these are characteristics of the lower plane of nature.[3]

Many of us, when confronted with an imperfection or personality flaw in another, have attempted to eradicate those imperfections. Sometimes those attempts are accompanied by anger and hostility that are born in the heat of the moment, yet the negative effects on a relationship can last years. This is the typical reaction for the simple reason that the lower nature alone does not possess the level of perception needed to see past the human flaws and envision the 'latent virtues' that we are told exist in every human soul.

The animal nature reacts to evil or imperfection as a threat to the physical well-being of the individual by either attempting to destroy the threat or running away from it.

The human nature reacts to an evil or imperfection that threatens a world created by the mind by trying to destroy the evil or imperfection or by running away from it.

Only the sin (evil or imperfection)-covering eye of the spiritual nature has the capacity to envision the perfection or the good in every individual or situation and work to build up that good or perfection. While the spiritual nature works in conjunction with the valuable contributions of the lower natures, it is the spiritual nature that has the farthest reaching vision. Without this vision the propensity of the lower natures to fight evil or imperfection goes unchecked and inevitably results in unproductive or even destructive behaviour. (A detailed explanation of our three natures, as 'Abdu'l-Bahá described them, is included in chapter 10, 'Coming Home to Our Spiritual Nature'.)

In the following quotation, 'Abdu'l-Bahá describes the choice that every individual faces:

> But on the other hand, when man does not open his mind and heart to the blessing of the spirit, but turns his soul towards the material side, towards the bodily part of his nature, then he is fallen from his high place and he becomes inferior to the inhabitants of the lower animal kingdom. In this case the man is in a sorry plight! For if the spiritual qualities of the soul, open to the breath of the Divine Spirit, are never used, they become atrophied, enfeebled, and at last incapable; whilst the soul's material qualities alone being exercised, they become terribly powerful – and the unhappy, misguided man becomes more savage, more unjust, more vile, more cruel, more malevolent than the lower animals themselves. All his aspirations and desires being strengthened

by the lower side of the soul's nature, he becomes more and more brutal, until his whole being is in no way superior to that of the beasts that perish. Men such as this, plan to work evil, to hurt and to destroy; they are entirely without the spirit of Divine compassion, for the celestial quality of the soul has been dominated by that of the material. **If, on the contrary, the spiritual nature of the soul has been so strengthened that it holds the material side in subjection, then does the man approach the Divine; his humanity becomes so glorified that the virtues of the Celestial Assembly are manifested in him; he radiates the Mercy of God, he stimulates the spiritual progress of mankind, for he becomes a lamp to show light on their path.**[4]

So, if we again consider the question 'What happens when "the willingness to fight against evils" is the standard used "to judge a person's moral worth"?', we see that people can begin to consider fault-finding or backbiting as acceptable and the result is **spiritual murder**. These may seem harsh words, and potentially excessive, yet this is just what Bahá'u'lláh describes:

> That seeker should also regard backbiting as grievous error, and keep himself aloof from its dominion, inasmuch as backbiting **quencheth the light of the heart, and extinguisheth the life of the soul.**[5]

He doesn't say we will have a bad day; He says the life of our soul will be extinguished. And when the light of our heart has been quenched or put out, for some this could lead to a slippery slope from which it becomes easy to justify all manner of evils, including actual, physical murder.

A horrifying case in point is the Nazis' attempt to eradicate the Jewish people in Europe. Long before the extermination camps were built a systematic campaign of incremental, dehumanizing acts that were tantamount to mental and spiritual murder was inflicted on the Jewish people. For example, a propaganda film was made showing Jews running through the streets and in the next frame the images of humans were replaced by those of rats.

The passages below suggest lines of action that can help us overcome the enormously destructive human tendencies of fault-finding and backbiting.

On no subject are the Bahá'í teachings more emphatic than on the necessity to abstain from fault-finding and backbiting while being ever eager to discover and root out our own faults and overcome our own failings.[6]

The Universal House of Justice suggests that you call to mind the admonitions found in our writings on the need to overlook the shortcomings of others, to forgive and conceal their misdeeds, not to expose their bad qualities, but to search for and affirm their praiseworthy ones, and endeavour to be always forbearing, patient, and merciful.[7]

It is important, of course, to be very specific about what is meant by 'building the good'. Within an interaction with another person we may perceive a negative quality, such as selfishness, and our first inclination is to destroy what we see. Immediately we can recognize that our perception has been generated by our lower natures and that we need a higher perception that can only come from our spiritual nature. This isn't going to be easy because our lower natures will be telling us that the problem lies entirely with the other person.

One possible remedy is to choose a conscious act of service towards that person that is motivated by a corresponding divine virtue, such as selflessness or generosity. By doing this we are asking our spiritual nature to take charge of the situation by calling its powers into play. The result is the building of the good in both the giver and the receiver of the act of service.

We can only imagine what a future society will look and feel like when it is free of the omnipresent pollution of backbiting, criticism and fault-finding. Fortunately, there is no need to wait until the world changes. We can take into our own hands the quality of our individual worlds.

So, what do we do? Certainly we do **not** make war on criticism, fault-finding and backbiting. Rather, here's what 'Abdu'l-Bahá has to say on the subject:

. . . the Cause of the Ancient Beauty is the very essence of love . . . existing only that all may become . . . servants one to another, adore one another, bless one another, praise one another; that each one may loose his tongue and extol the rest without exception, each one voice his gratitude to all the rest; that all should lift up their eyes to the horizon of glory, and remember that they are linked to the Holy Threshold; that they should see nothing but good in one another, hear nothing but praise of one another, and speak no word of one another save only to praise.[8]

The solution, as Shoghi Effendi also intimates in the following quotation, is to move from a culture of criticism to a culture of encouragement, not only in the way we treat others but in how we treat ourselves. Backbiting is a grievous crime against humanity and each of us is part of that humanity. It is no less a grievous offence to engage in endless criticism and backbiting against our own self.

> You are quite correct in your understanding of the importance of avoiding backbiting; such conduct strikes at the very unity of the Bahá'í community. In a letter written to an individual believer on behalf of the Guardian it is stated: 'If we are better, if we show love, patience, and understanding of the weakness of others, if we seek to never criticize but rather encourage, others will do likewise, and we can really help the Cause through our example and spiritual strength.' [9]

The challenge is to make the transition from a culture of criticism to a culture of encouragement without stopping at some illusory midpoint of silence. It is not enough to be silent and refrain from criticism. We must look carefully for those sometimes hard-to-notice small triumphs of the human spirit, acknowledge them to our brothers and sisters and demonstrate to them that we notice and are appreciative of what they offer. The initial reaction many of us might have is that nobody could live such a life but then 'Abdu'l-Bahá stands before us with the majestic example of His own life that expands our perception of what is possible.

Ron, one of the authors, recently participated in a class in which the teacher related a story about her pre-teen daughter. The mother was in the habit of criticizing her daughter in an effort to improve her behaviour. The more she criticized, the worse her daughter's behaviour became. In desperation, the teacher decided to heed the wisdom of spiritual guidance and ceased entirely criticizing her daughter. Instead, she praised and encouraged her daughter at every opportunity. She joked in class about how many times she'd had to bite her lip but she did not return to her old habit of criticizing her daughter's behaviour. She applied discipline where her daughter's behaviour called for it but offered no criticism. Slowly but surely her daughter's behaviour and attitude improved.

Ron would have had a hard time understanding how this metamorphosis had occurred if his wife and he had not had a similar experience with their daughter. What they noticed when they stopped criticizing and began encouraging their daughter was that she became less angry and more self-confident. Eventually she began to ask their advice on how to handle situations and problems, instead of retreating into an angry shell. It dawned on her parents that the wonderful, frank conversations they were now having with her occurred only because she felt safe. She knew that they would not criticize. The safer she felt, the more effective those family consultations were. This, says Ron, is one of many examples of an experience in which he discovered the practical wisdom of the sacred guidance only after he had obeyed and followed through on enacting it.

After all, this is how it works we are told. We are limited to our best guess in any moment but out of trust and faith we apply spiritual principles in our daily lives and we then learn as we observe the consequences of our behaviour. From this we can modify and adjust, act and continue to learn.

If we do not attempt to build the good in ourselves, we can fall into a dangerous state of mind. If we believe, as most of the world does, that it is possible to make war on evil, then it is possible we will make war on our own selves for engaging in backbiting, fault-finding or any number of negative behaviours. We could demonize ourselves, making it more difficult for us to perceive the good within us that needs to be both recognized and nurtured.

If we feel fear about ourselves because we have been among those who have mistreated us, how do we gain a desire to investigate our own reality? The starting point of self-healing is to realize that we are created noble, in the image (spiritual reality) of God, and have the ability to reflect the attributes of God.

If our problem is impatience, for example, then we direct our attention towards building up the attribute of patience. As we make such a concentrated effort, even in the most insignificant actions of the day, we might practise deep breathing or saying prayers aloud very, very slowly. These are two actions that could actually assist us to cultivate what we are seeking and are also productive, rather than defaulting to the destructive reaction of making war on ourselves. As in every war, not only combatants suffer injury but so do innocent bystanders. As it happens, these are most likely to be the people in the world that we care about the most.

To recap: According to the guidance we have considered, if we engage in backbiting, we are engaged in the spiritual murder of another person, as well as our self. We possess the 'worst human quality'. We have 'committed the greatest sin'. We have participated in impeding the happiness of the world and contributed to the misery of mankind.

And here is a vision of what the world would look like if we could get rid of backbiting:

> If some means were devised so that the doors of backbiting were shut eternally and each one of the believers unsealed his lips in praise of others, then the Teachings of His Holiness Bahá'u'lláh would spread, the hearts be illumined, the spirits glorified, and the human world would attain to everlasting felicity.[10]

What a vision of hope this is. Our contribution to it is well-defined and actually quite simple – as long as we're willing to have our spiritual nature claim its birthright and fulfil its purpose. What a powerful expression of the building of the good indeed.

At this time in human history, the stakes could not be higher. And it all depends upon each and every member of humanity addressing the essential sequential questions of human reality as they have been enumerated by the Universal House of Justice:

1) Who we are

2) To what purpose we exist

3) How we should act towards one another; and

4) How to apply these answers to our everyday behaviour

The next chapter attempts to answer the most perplexing question:

Why, after thousands of years and the sacrifices of the Manifestations of God and their devoted followers, have any attempts to answer these questions failed to bring the longed-for peace that all faiths anticipate and hope for?

It is not because of apathy on the part of humanity, nor any lack of effort or action towards trying to find answers. Instead, the problem seems to reside at the level at which those answers have been sought – that of our lower natures.

And these answers have undoubtedly proved elusive because of the second – and major – stumbling block on the path to investigating reality, about which 'Abdu'l-Bahá warned His listeners repeatedly and which the next chapter addresses in detail. It is blind imitation of the past – in our actions, our thinking and beliefs – that keeps the answers to those questions elusive, no matter how desperately we seek them. As we investigate reality, it's time to recognize where blind imitation gets in the way of doing that.

THE ILLNESS

Blind Imitation

The essence of all that We have revealed for thee is Justice, is for man to free himself from idle fancy and **imitation**, discern with the eye of oneness His glorious handiwork, and look into all things with a searching eye.[1]

Humanity is suffering terribly. We turn to the nightly news and see the last moments of a starving child or a soldier dying on the battlefield. That is the outward state of affairs and our inward condition is often no better. How did we get into such a mess?

Again, the letter of the Universal House of Justice of 19 November 1974 on material suffering has the answer:

> The principal cause of this suffering, which one can witness wherever one turns, is the corruption of human morals and the prevalence of prejudice, suspicion, hatred, untrustworthiness, selfishness and tyranny among men.[2]

And what is the cause of these inner spiritual deficits that have resulted in such widespread suffering? How the authors stumbled upon an answer to this question was sheer happenstance. About 28 years ago Ron was asked to give a talk. This was before the days when computer search software made research quick and easy, and as he prepared his topic, he had to rely on a huge book by James Heggie called *An Index of Quotations from the Bahá'í Sacred Writings* and another of his entitled *Bahá'í References to Judaism, Christianity and Islam*. Nothing caught his eye in this book until he came to the references on imitation and blind imitation.

Ron was stunned. Each subsequent quotation on the topic seemed more astounding than the last. The passages indicated that every single evil in the world, whether it be a problem between two people trying to live under one roof or seven billion people trying to live on one planet, can be attributed to blind imitation. What were previously thought to be a multiplicity of evils were, in fact, only symptoms of a single common root source of evil that has remained hidden from view.

The magnitude of this concept brought to mind an image of standing on the deck of a ship and seeing hundreds of icebergs of many sizes floating in the water. What was not visible was the reality that these hundreds of icebergs were outcroppings of a single, mammoth ice structure hidden from view below the surface of the ocean.

When Ron checked the sources for these references, he found that many were from *The Promulgation of Universal Peace*, the published collection of talks that had been given by 'Abdu'l-Bahá in 1912 while travelling in North America.

As he began a thorough, line-by-line reading of each talk with a pen and notebook at his side, Ron was astonished to discover that of the 139 talks of 'Abdu'l-Bahá recorded in *The Promulgation of Universal Peace,* given as He travelled from the east coast of North America to the west, more than 40 dealt with imitation, blind imitation and its remedy, the investigation of reality. More astonishing still was that in his 30 years as a Bahá'í, Ron had never attended a class or other study of this subject. It appeared that this consistent message of 'Abdu'l-Bahá had somehow been missed, to the extent that the words and concepts of 'imitation' or 'blind imitation' were not even listed as main subjects in the book's index.

'Abdu'l-Bahá had been a prisoner and an exile from the age of nine to the age of 64, when He was set free as a consequence of the Revolution of the Young Turks in 1908. As He set out on His extensive travels in the West in 1911, He was in constant pain, His feet having been frostbitten as He travelled across high mountains on His exile from Tehran as a child. He refused money from wealthy individuals that would have provided luxurious accommodation and travel. He refused to ride first class on trains and instead sat up all night crammed in with other passengers. He was surrounded every day by individuals He knew would betray Him in the future. These same individuals had plotted to prevent from accompanying Him on this journey the one person whose company would have brought Him the greatest happiness – his grandson, Shoghi Effendi. Given the hardships He willingly endured to undertake this trip, how could we not listen to what He had to tell us?

When Ron was invited to be a presenter at the annual winter school at Green Acre Bahá'í School in Maine, a place 'Abdu'l-Bahá had visited during His travels in North America, he was nervous because he now felt honour-bound to address the topic of blind imitation. The winter school typically attracted seasoned Bahá'ís who were very familiar with the writings of the Faith. Ron had visions of standing in front of 70 people who would break out in laughter when he mentioned blind imitation, imagining them saying, 'Oh, yes, we know all about that.' However, he dipped his feet in the water by cautiously writing a quotation on the blackboard:

The root cause of prejudice is _____.

He asked those in the class to help fill in the blank. After half an hour of guessing, no one had identified the correct answer.

The answer was blind imitation. The following is the complete quotation he shared that day as his reference:

> And the breeding-ground of all these tragedies is prejudice: prejudice of race and nation, of religion, of political opinion; and the **root cause** of prejudice is blind imitation of the past – imitation in religion, in racial attitudes, in national bias, in politics. So long as this aping of the past persisteth, just so long will the foundations of the social order be blown to the four winds, just so long will humanity be continually exposed to direst peril.[3]

Ron remembers feeling more scared after the class than he had before it. He had secretly hoped that people would know all about blind imitation and he could turn his attention towards writing books for children.

But being a Bahá'í seems to be all about attempting what seems impossible, feeling called upon to accomplish tasks that we also feel inadequate to perform, whether it be serving on a spiritual assembly, the administrative body of the Faith, offering our service in faraway and unfamiliar places or opening our lips to acknowledge and pay tribute to divine mysteries. Despite his fears, Ron's heartfelt love for 'Abdu'l-Bahá led him on a 28-year journey that has finally resulted in his contribution to this book.

Diane's path is different. Perhaps as a gift from her parents, she came to believe that humanity had the potential to be a greater force for good than was being manifested in the world. When she learned of the Bahá'í Faith, she recognized it as the means by which this could be accomplished.

Not long after she recognized herself as a Bahá'í, Diane read a small booklet called 'Becoming Your True Self' by Daniel C. Jordan. It described the importance of investigating reality for ourselves, especially our own, truest reality.

'This is why I became a Bahá'í,' she realized when she finished reading it.

She soon went to work for the National Spiritual Assembly of the Bahá'ís of the United States at its National Center in Wilmette, Illinois. While knowledge of the developments in the Faith worldwide and the uplifting words delivered at the House of Worship in Wilmette brought her great joy, she felt no closer to being a better and more effective force for good herself than she had previously. She felt that there was a gap in her understanding of how to implement the Faith in her day-to-day life.

Circumstances led her to serve at Green Acre Bahá'í School in Eliot, Maine, where she met Dr Mary Tomanio, discovered the work of Marian Lippitt and, consequently, met Ron Tomanio. He had also been influenced by these two dynamic women, each of whom was a very dedicated student of the teachings of the Bahá'í Faith.

Ron's Green Acre winter school experience led him to ask Diane to join forces with him in finding a way to share this information with others. As they began, all they knew was that this subject of the disease of blind imitation, and its remedy, the investigation of reality, were extremely important to 'Abdu'l-Bahá. As they explored the Bahá'í writings and began to share their discoveries with others, they learned that Bahá'u'lláh had also identified these as important subjects that would have a significant impact on the development of human potential as a source of building good in the world.

Phyllis's story began in childhood when she discovered that those messengers who had brought divine guidance – Christ, Moses, Buddha, Krishna, Muhammad and others – had all brought the promise of a time of fulfilment and the unity of all God's children. She recognized that the truth of this was an important light to keep in view in an increasingly dark world. She also felt that the way we could recognize that eternal, indestructible light would be in the lives of those who loved it so much that they were willing to let it transform them. Such souls had sought the path that the saints had always sought, and their subsequent actions – their very presence in the world – had offered a source of light to others.

After a turbulent, sometimes dangerous adolescence, and determined to keep seeking that light, Phyllis arrived, through a series of events, on Marian Lippitt's doorstep. Her host, then in her eighties, embodied that light, diffusing it all around her with unbounded love and encouragement.

Eventually, Phyllis learned more about 'Abdu'l-Bahá, whose example inspired Marian and Bahá'ís in every part of the world to follow a path on which divine light was leading the way to peace. She learned, too, about Bahá'u'lláh, who had renewed the brilliance of that light in the world and kept the promises made by those other Manifestations of God she loved.

Phyllis witnessed Marian's life as a living act of love aimed at helping souls learn together how to move beyond the prison of blind imitation of the past and allow the Light of God to call forth the most spiritually motivated possibilities from their noblest selves. That, the Bahá'í teachings described, was the path by which God was guiding humanity towards unity and peace.

In order to understand the significance and effects of blind imitation, the authors have taken a sampling of quotations about it (which appear in their entirety in appendix 3) and turned them into short, action phrases, to emphasize the full impact and effect of this root cause of all prejudice and underlying cause of evil in the world:

- Imitations of ancestral beliefs have hindered the progress of humanity for thousands of years.

- Through imitation we find points of disagreement and division among religions, the (true) foundation of which is oneness.

- One who holds to imitation is lacking in love for humanity and manifests hatred and bigotry.

- Imitation produces enmity and strife, jealousy, war and bloodshed.

- Imitation prevents the refreshment provided by the down-pouring of rain of mercy, and illumination by the rays of the Sun of Truth.

- Imitation destroys the foundation of religion.

- Imitation extinguishes the spirituality of the human world.

- Imitation deprives us of the knowledge of God.

- Imitation is the cause of the victory of infidelity and material-ism over religion.

- Imitation is the denial of Divinity and the law of revelation.

- Imitation refuses Prophethood and rejects the Kingdom of God.

- So long as imitations remain, the oneness of the world of humanity is impossible.

- Blind imitations have invariably become the cause of bitter-ness and hatred and have filled the world with darkness and violence of war.

- The greatest cause of bereavement and disheartening in the world of humanity is ignorance based upon blind imitation. It is due to this that wars and battles prevail; from this cause hatred and animosity arise continually among mankind.

- As long as imitation persists, strife and contention will destroy the purpose of religion and make love and fellowship impossible.

- The root cause of prejudice is blind imitation of the past – imitation in religion, in racial attitudes, in national bias, in politics.

- Blind imitation stunts the mind.

- Imitation prevents focus on new principles, which are the light of this time and very spirit of this age.

- Imitations are destroyers of human foundations established by the heavenly Educators.

- As long as imitation persists, humanity will find neither happiness nor rest nor composure.

The above have been drawn from just a small sampling of passages on this topic that can be found in the Bahá'í writings.

Beyond their own spiritual transformation, Bahá'ís also care deeply about the inherent potential in each and every soul. They long to hasten the day when the oneness of humankind is realized, yet, as 'Abdu'l-Bahá has said, 'So long as these imitations remain, the oneness of the world of humanity is impossible.'[4]

Without true investigation of reality, the realization of the oneness of religion is also impossible. In 2005 an extraordinary document, *One Common Faith*, was produced under the supervision of the Universal House of Justice. The opening paragraph states:

> There is every reason for confidence that the period of history now opening will be far more receptive to efforts to spread Bahá'u'lláh's message than was the case in the century just ended. All the signs indicate that a sea change in human consciousness is under way.[5]

Perhaps the first wave of this sea change appeared in the wake of 'Abdu'l-Bahá's visit to the shores of North America where He emphasized the vital importance of the investigation of reality. *One Common Faith* boldly declares the underlying reality of the world's religions to be one but the corrosive effects of imitation prevent a realization of the awareness of their common foundation. 'Abdu'l-Bahá says:

If we investigate these foundations, we discover much ground for agreement, but if we consider the imitations of forms and ancestral beliefs, we find points of disagreement and division; for these imitations differ, while the sources and foundations are one and the same.[6]

Imitation destroys the foundation of religion . . .[7]

The result of the investigation of reality is actually seeing that God is one, humankind is one and religion is one. When Ron's Bahá'í community studied *One Common Faith* together, the participants found that the experience altered their use of language, as drawing any distinctions between 'us' and 'them' was no longer possible.

In fact, every issue that most people care about, whether it be war, the spread of hatred, ignorance, all forms of prejudice, the advancement of civilization or human degradation and suffering can only be addressed on the superficial level of symptoms if we cannot rid ourselves of blind imitation. The result of an individual or a society being held captive by imitation is that, as with icebergs, every situation is perceived only on the most superficial level. The underlying reality remains hidden.

How would we feel if we walked into an emergency room with a broken arm and the doctor gave us a painkiller and sent us home without setting our arm? Now, maybe the painkiller is needful, at the moment, but the cause of the pain, the broken arm, must be addressed.

The premise of this book is that the underlying cause of what truly ails the individual and the world can never be eliminated unless human souls find the will to recognize the error in blind imitation and to relinquish it in favour of, and in service to, truth.

With an understanding of the illness, imitation, we are ready to learn more about the remedy, the investigation of reality.

3

THE REMEDY

Investigating Reality

'Abdu'l-Bahá has not only identified blind imitation as the root cause of the deadly illness that afflicts humanity but has also specified the remedy: the investigation of reality. How important is this principle of investigation? When 'Abdu'l-Bahá came to the West in 1912 to share the truths revealed by His father, an interviewer asked Him,

> Will you state the tenets of your faith?

> *Answer:* First, investigate reality. Man must leave imitation and seek reality. The contemporaneous religious beliefs differ because of their allegiance to dogma. It is necessary, therefore, to abandon imitations and seek their fundamental reality.[1]

'Abdu'l-Bahá states that this prospect of investigation is primary: 'First, investigate reality.'

He also qualifies this by stating that we must leave off imitation in order to do this: 'Man must leave imitation and seek reality.' He further stated:

> So long as these imitations remain, the oneness of the world of humanity is impossible.[2]

> If we abandon these timeworn blind imitations and investigate reality, all of us will be unified.[3]

This means each of us has to independently investigate truth or reality for ourselves. In the chapters that follow we offer a starting place, a first step in the process, in which the gift of 'Abdu'l-Bahá's life offers a model of how to investigate truth.

> First among the great principles revealed by Him is that of the investigation of reality. The meaning is that every individual member of humankind is exhorted and commanded to set aside superstitious beliefs, traditions and blind imitation of ancestral forms in religion and investigate reality for himself. Inasmuch as the fundamental reality is one, all religions and nations of the world will become one through the investigation of reality. **The announcement of this principle is not found in any of the sacred Books of the past.**[4]

We live in a truly amazing time. It is now possible for us to become aware that the source of all evil, blind imitation, can be eliminated through the investigation of reality. The process of eliminating blind imitation in our lives takes place reaction by reaction. It is also enhanced through the experience of undertaking continually more complex acts of chosen service. (Further explanation of what is meant by acts of service follows in the next chapter.)

Inspired by the life example of 'Abdu'l-Bahá, we can remove the veils of illusions that obscure the presence of our unique and indescribably powerful true self. Since we have been given the principle of the investigation of reality, it follows that humankind must also have evolved to the point that we can use this concept successfully. For the first time, the realization of human oneness, in reality, is within our grasp. And each of us is invited to discover our unique, true identity as a soul, as well as our unique purpose and our unique way of solving problems.

> Happy are those who spend their days in gaining knowledge, in discovering the secrets of nature, and in penetrating the subtleties of pure truth! Woe to those who are contented with ignorance, whose hearts are gladdened by thoughtless imitation, who have fallen into the lowest depths of ignorance and foolishness, and who have wasted their lives![5]

> God has given man the eye of investigation by which he may see and recognize truth. He has endowed man with ears that he may hear the message of reality and conferred upon him the gift of reason by

which he may discover things for himself. This is his endowment and equipment for the investigation of reality. Man is not intended to see through the eyes of another, hear through another's ears nor comprehend with another's brain. **Each human creature has individual endowment, power and responsibility in the creative plan of God.** Therefore, depend upon your own reason and judgement and adhere to the outcome of your own investigation; otherwise, you will be utterly submerged in the sea of ignorance and deprived of all the bounties of God. Turn to God, supplicate humbly at His threshold, seeking assistance and confirmation, that God may rend asunder the veils that obscure your vision. Then will your eyes be filled with illumination, face to face you will behold the reality of God and your heart become completely purified from the dross of ignorance, reflecting the glories and bounties of the Kingdom.

Holy souls are like soil which has been ploughed and tilled with much earnest labour, the thorns and thistles cast aside and all weeds uprooted. Such soil is most fruitful, and the harvest from it will prove full and plenteous. In this same way man must free himself from the weeds of ignorance, thorns of superstitions and thistles of imitations that he may discover reality in the harvests of true knowledge. Otherwise, the discovery of reality is impossible, contention and divergence of religious belief will always remain, and mankind, like ferocious wolves, will rage and attack each other in hatred and antagonism. We supplicate God that He may destroy the veils which limit our vision and that these becloudings, which darken the way of the manifestation of the shining lights, may be dispelled in order that the effulgent Sun of Reality may shine forth. We implore and invoke God, seeking His assistance and confirmation. Man is a child of God, most noble, lofty and beloved by God, his Creator. Therefore, he must ever strive that the divine bounties and virtues bestowed upon him may prevail and control him. Just now the soil of human hearts seems like black earth, but in the innermost substance of this dark soil there are thousands of fragrant flowers latent. We must endeavour to cultivate and awaken these potentialities, discover the secret treasure in this very mine and depository of God, bring forth these resplendent powers long hidden in human hearts. Then will the glories of both worlds be blended and increased and the quintessence of human existence be made manifest.

We must not be content with simply following a certain course because we find our fathers pursued that course. **It is the duty of everyone to investigate reality, and investigation of reality by another will not do for us.** If all in the world were rich and one man poor, of what use are these riches to that man? If all the world be virtuous and a man steeped in vice, what good results are forthcoming from him? If all the world be resplendent and a man blind, where are his benefits? If all the world be in plenty and a man hungry, what sustenance does he derive? Therefore, every man must be an investigator for himself. Ideas and beliefs left by his fathers and ancestors as a heritage will not suffice, for adherence to these are but imitations, and imitations have ever been a cause of disappointment and misguidance. Be investigators of reality that you may attain the verity of truth and life.

You have asked why it was necessary for the soul that was from God to make this journey back to God? Would you like to understand the reality of this question just as I teach it, or do you wish to hear it as the world teaches it? For if I should answer you according to the latter way, this would be but imitation and would not make the subject clear.[6]

In Nader Saiedi's book *Gate of the Heart: Understanding the Writings of the Báb*, the author offers his insights into a Tablet of the Báb called the Epistle of Justice. The author writes:

> These words of the Báb, then, are the words of justice, and His Revelation is nothing less than that long-awaited advent of true justice in the world.[7]

For justice to be the hallmark of a new, emerging world civilization, it must be established by the individuals making up that civilization. But how is justice manifested on an individual level in this new age? Shoghi Effendi tells us that

> The greatest need it seems everywhere inside the Cause is to impress upon the friends the need for love among them. There is a tendency to mix up the functions of the Administration and try to apply it in individual relationships, which is abortive, because the Assembly is a nascent House of Justice and is supposed to administer, according to the Teachings, the affairs of the community. But individuals toward each other are governed by love, unity, forgiveness and a sin-covering

eye. Once the friends grasp this they will get along much better, but they keep playing Spiritual Assembly to each other and expect the Assembly to behave like an individual . . .[8]

The coming new civilization will have divinely-ordained institutions to dispense justice between individuals, which will allow the individual to be 'governed by love, unity, forgiveness and a sin-covering eye'. Clearly we are not to act either outwardly or inwardly as anyone's judge, jury or executioner. So the question remains, how is justice practised on an individual level in this new age and why are we bringing up this question in a chapter on the investigation of reality?

We have just read the above quotation that explains:

Man is not intended to see through the eyes of another, hear through another's ears nor comprehend with another's brain. Each human creature has individual endowment, power and responsibility in the creative plan of God.[9]

A new basic human right has been bestowed on humankind: the right of every individual to investigate reality for himself or herself. We maintain that the investigation of reality is the manifestation of the attribute of justice in the world on an individual level. The beginning of the process of the personal investigation of reality is, as 'Abdu'l-Bahá describes, to see with our own eyes and hear with our own ears.

In the following Hidden Word Bahá'u'lláh links this concept of seeing with our own eyes with the concept of justice:

O Son of Spirit! The best beloved of all things in My sight is Justice; turn not away therefrom if thou desirest Me, and neglect it not that I may confide in thee. By its aid thou shalt see with thine own eyes and not through the eyes of others, and shalt know of thine own knowledge and not through the knowledge of thy neighbour. Ponder this in thy heart; how it behoveth thee to be. Verily justice is My gift to thee and the sign of My loving-kindness. Set it then before thine eyes.[10]

In addition, we have seen in chapter 2 that Bahá'u'lláh says:

The essence of all that We have revealed for thee is Justice, is for man to free himself from idle fancy and imitation, discern with the eye of oneness His glorious handiwork, and look into all things with a searching eye.[11]

These passages suggest that there is a direct connection between the investigation of reality, seeing with our own eyes, and justice. Our first step in manifesting justice as individuals is to see with our own eyes and not blindly imitate the perceptions of others.

By now it will have become evident that the investigation of reality is a sacred and deeply spiritual responsibility. Individual, independent investigation allows us to come to see each other as 'Abdu'l-Bahá sees us and treat each other as He would treat us: as unique, valuable and well-loved servants of God.

Let's look again at the verse that opened chapter 2 on blind imitation:

The essence of all that We have revealed for thee is **Justice**, is for man to free himself from idle fancy and imitation, discern with the eye of oneness His glorious handiwork, and look into all things with a searching eye.[12]

Justice, the cherished goal that can benefit every individual in every land, can only be achieved if we are able to free ourselves from idle fancy and imitation. Justice will be realized when the investigation of reality takes its place as a most essential of basic human rights.

The next chapter explores an action step in the process, one inspired by the example of 'Abdu'l-Bahá, who defines action as a necessary component in 'the attainment of any object', including the investigation of reality:

The attainment of any object is conditioned upon knowledge, volition, and action. Unless these three conditions are forthcoming, there is no execution or accomplishment.[13]

It is incumbent upon every man of insight and understanding to strive to translate that which hath been written into reality and **action** . . .

That one indeed is a man who, today, dedicateth himself to the service of the entire human race.[14]

THE TWO SERVICE QUESTIONS

A Suggested Action Step for the Investigation of Reality

What profit is there in agreeing that universal friendship is good, and talking of the solidarity of the human race as a grand idea? Unless these thoughts are translated into the world of **action**, they are useless . . . If actions took the place of words, the world's misery would soon be changed into comfort.[1]

One holy **action** maketh the world of earth highest paradise.[2]

The day of service is now come.[3]

Confidence is patiently built as the friends engage in progressively more complex and demanding acts of service.[4]

The investigation of reality is not merely an intellectual exercise accomplished through the memorization of certain facts while sitting in an easy chair. As the quotations that ended the previous chapter emphasized, it requires action, accompanied by the willingness to carry out those actions.

> Knowledge is the first step; resolve, the second step; **action, its fulfilment**, is the third step.[5]

Over time the authors have found that the individual's ongoing process of investigating reality is greatly assisted by what we call the two service questions, an approach inspired by the example of 'Abdu'l-Bahá:

1) At this moment in time, what is the act of service I am capable

of giving that the other person is capable of receiving?

2) At this moment in time, what is the act of service I am capable of receiving that the other person is capable of giving?

These are questions that we ask ourselves and not anyone else. We have been given the right by God, for the first time in history, to investigate reality **for ourselves**, which means we do not have to blindly imitate the thought processes of any other person.

Naturally, this privilege is not a licence to become arrogant or deaf to the advice of others. Asking questions of ourselves and others is actually a profound act of humility.

Asking inner questions is an essential part of the process of receiving divine inspiration. Doing this also signifies that we have been endowed by the Creator with nobility and self-worth that we can access and that we deserve to have a seat of truth at the table of knowledge.

The end result of knowledge is action, and for a servant of God, that is an act of service. This means that our inner questions, plus the questions we ask others, ought to ultimately result in acts of service.

The discovery of knowledge and truth – the investigation of reality – begins with asking questions:

1) At this moment in time, what is the act of service I am capable of **giving** that the other person is capable of **receiving**?

2) At this moment in time, what is the act of service I am capable of **receiving** that the other person is capable of **giving**?

Every human interaction is either an act of giving or an act of receiving. By asking questions that encompass both giving and receiving, our sensitivity to our own needs and the needs of others is increased daily. These two elements are equally important because giving depends on someone willing and capable of receiving from us and receiving depends on someone willing and capable of giving to us.

When we share this concept in classes, we always ask people to raise their hands if they are more comfortable giving than receiving, or conversely, more comfortable receiving than giving. We then ask all the people who are better at giving to stand on one side of the room and all the people who are more comfortable receiving to stand on the other.

It never fails that at least nine out of ten people are more comfortable giving. We then ask that the two sides join up. We then wait for the 'aha moment' when they realize that it doesn't matter how good or comfortable they are with giving if there is no one comfortable or good at receiving. Both sides stand on opposite and distant sides of the room – a living metaphor for how distant we sometimes feel inside, even towards people we love very much. We think the reason for the imbalance is that we probably feel safer in our ability to control what we give.

From the path of our own experience, we wish to reassure you that with continued consistent use of the two service questions over time, it is possible to create a healthy balance between one's ability to give and one's ability to receive. Successful relationships and true service, whether in our personal or professional lives, depend on our ability to be equally proficient at both giving and receiving.

I	We	I
	Δ	
Giving →	Balance/Intimacy	← Receiving

The diagram above illustrates how, when we move toward balance, we can make an intimate connection with others. This is the connection, the 'we' that we all crave. For example, we speak; we listen. We give love; we receive love. Over time, as we align our actions with the example of 'Abdu'l-Bahá, we begin to achieve this balance.

Balance is a key concept in the Bahá'í writings. 'Balance' is one of the titles of the Manifestation of God and is also used to describe the Covenant of Bahá'u'lláh. Balance is also cited as a key to physical health by 'Abdu'l-Bahá.[6]

The continued use of the two service questions gradually helps each of us achieve balance between all our powers, faculties and spiritual attributes, known and unknown. That's because each of these powers, faculties and attributes has a giving and receiving component.

In addition, every attribute, power and faculty we possess, both known and unknown, will be brought into balance as we strive to balance the service acts of giving and receiving. Any imbalance in this process causes a distortion of vision, which affects our decision-making and could result in blind imitation. We might be seeing with our own eyes but our eyesight is distorted. How can we investigate reality if that is the case?

We have also found it to be quite common for individuals in an intimate relationship to experience at times the feeling that they are a million miles from one another. We ask them to look first at their ability to give and receive to see if that is in balance. A serious imbalance in our ability to give and receive affects in a negative way all our relationships, including our relationship with God.

The closer we get to a state of balance, the closer we get to the ideal of moderation in all things. We live in an age where the concept of 'enough' is in danger of being lost. We work too much, play too much, eat too much – or the opposite is true. In short, our ability to give and receive is out of balance, affecting all aspects of our life. If all our actions in this world are acts of service, with both acts of giving and receiving equally valued, we can achieve a state of moderation.

Ron recalls an experience he had in his early twenties that helped illuminate this concept for him:

> One year during the annual New York Bahá'í Summer School the teacher of the class, Charlie Wragg, seemed to have an answer for every question I asked, and it became my goal to stump him. I awoke one morning with a question for which I was sure he wouldn't have an answer. We were staying at the men's dorm and when I went into the communal bathroom, Charlie was standing in front of the mirror in his underwear with his face covered in shaving cream.
>
> 'Ha, ha,' I thought. 'This is my chance to finally elicit an "I don't know".' I said, 'Charlie, if God is all-merciful, why do we need to pay attention to always doing the right thing? Won't God forgive us anyway?'
>
> Charlie responded without pausing a moment to think or put down his razor: 'God is all-merciful and all-forgiving but you have to develop the spiritual capacity to be able to **receive** that mercy and forgiveness.'

We all receive requests from friends to pray for someone who is sick or out of work or going through relationship problems. We ask God to give them healing or assistance of some kind. The problem is not that

God needs to get better at giving but we need to get better at receiving. Try changing the prayer by asking God to help you strengthen your ability to achieve balance between giving and receiving.

In this world or the next, we will eventually attain an inner balance, a point at which giving and receiving will become one. We will experience the intimate presence of all our fellow servants and we will experience the presence of God. But this can be a long journey on the path of service and patience is required.

> The steed of this Valley is patience; without patience the wayfarer on this journey will reach nowhere and attain no goal. Nor should he ever be downhearted; if he strive for a hundred thousand years and yet fail to behold the beauty of the Friend, he should not falter.[7]

Eventually the disparity between giving and receiving fades away and they become one, just as the superficial differences of personality fade away between servants of God and we attain to the realization of the oneness of humankind. Again, 'Abdu'l-Bahá offers an example.

Ron remembers Dr Stanwood Cobb sharing the story of how he once went with 'Abdu'l-Bahá to see Stanwood's distinguished father and how he was anxious that 'Abdu'l-Bahá educate his father about Bahá'u'lláh's Revelation. During the meeting, however, Stanwood's father poured out his ideas and his heart to 'Abdu'l-Bahá, who did nothing but smile, listen intently and offer his loving presence. When they were leaving, Stanwood later described, his father told him that 'Abdu'l-Bahá was the wisest man he had ever met and thanked Stanwood profusely for arranging the meeting.

What actually happened? Did 'Abdu'l-Bahá receive or did He give? Or had giving and receiving become one – a perfect balance?

> The Revelation of Bahá'u'lláh is designed to **create a balance** between the spiritual and material so that this power can work within proper channels to introduce the most wonderful age in human history.[8]

As we contemplate the role of balance, we can also remember that everything in the world is in a state of constant change. Everything is either growing or dying and nothing stays the same. 'Abdu'l-Bahá confirms this:

Know thou that nothing which exists remains in a state of repose – that is to say, all things are in motion. Everything is either growing or declining . . .[9]

1) **At this moment in time**, what is the act of service I am capable of giving that the other person is capable of receiving?

2) **At this moment in time**, what is the act of service I am capable of receiving that the other person is capable of giving?

At this moment in time, a person may not be capable of a particular act of service. Just because we could not do a particular act of service yesterday speaks only to our state of being yesterday and does not necessarily hold true today.

At this moment also makes us aware that we might be capable of an even greater act of service today than yesterday and we need to guard against the natural lower-nature inclination of maintaining the status quo or we could end up **blindly imitating** what we did yesterday day after day. In the framework of these two questions, **capable** is a constantly changing state of being.

Conversely, we will have moments of enormous stress caused by the tests and difficulties of life. That means that yesterday we might have felt on top of the mountain but today we feel like we are standing in a deep valley and cannot even see the top of the mountain.

It is up to each of us to ultimately decide what we are **capable** of giving and receiving. We suggest that **capable** implies that which constitutes a wise or healthy action on our part, determined by the circumstances at this particular moment in time.

For example, it is always a good idea to help people in need. However, if we render so much help that our family starves, the extent of that act was unwise and unhealthy. Likewise, we would not want to take for ourselves the last morsel of food from another starving family.

There is never any reason to beat ourselves up if we want to do something but can't quite summon the strength to do it. Tomorrow is another day. Self-inflicted wounds will only make it more difficult for us to reach our aspirations.

Our ability to choose acts of service will be refined by our experience. Each of us is the only one who can decide if we are capable of a particular act of service at this moment. Living a life based on other people's expectations of what we may be capable of is living someone else's life and not our own. In doing this, we are blindly imitating someone else who resides in this world or the next.

The two service questions are intended to be directed inward, inviting us to give or receive an act of service. These inner questions can only be adequately answered and then translated into acts of service by our spiritual nature, with its enormous potential for creativity.

One might think that for some simple situations the inner questions could be adequately answered by our lower nature. For example: Someone spills a glass of water and we perform an act of service by mopping it up. But is it an act of service? Was the act performed with love in our heart or was it performed with concealed anger and thoughts of 'Why is this person so messy and clumsy?'

We believe that only the spiritual nature can perform genuine acts of service. The material act itself remains an empty vessel of potential that only rises to the level of an act of service when it is filled with love or another attribute of God.

Getting the sequence right is difficult because we breathe the air of this material world in a particularly materialistic age. When we introduce the two service questions in a class there is always confusion at first.

'What do you mean, I should ask myself what is the appropriate act of service?' The confusion exists primarily because we must first reflect on what attribute of God a relationship needs. This is not solely a rational, mechanical process – in fact, a 180 degree change in focus is needed. It's most effective not to even think about the outer act until we feel prompted by the call of our own heart as to what divine quality is needed. When that is known, we find that the act of service will flow naturally from the needed attribute. The quality of God becomes the source of the outer act.

Imagine wanting to send a thank-you card by regular mail. Would we rush to the post office and put a stamp on the envelope without doing what is most important – writing sincere words of love and gratitude? Once we allow ourselves to feel the attributes of love and gratitude, our words or an act of service will flow naturally, and will also reach the heart of the recipient. The language spoken between hearts is an act of service, the language of the spiritual nature.

We have previously reflected on the reality that the source of all the evil situations that humans create is blind imitation. In light of this, perhaps a helpful question to ask ourselves in any situation is, 'What act of service can we give or receive that is inspired by the example of 'Abdu'l-Bahá?' Reflecting on the divine qualities that are behind the example of 'Abdu'l-Bahá's actions might assist us in answering this question.

There are both outer and inner acts of service. An example of an inner act of service could be holding someone in prayerful awareness. Sometimes when emotions are raw an inner act of service is all that we will be capable of giving at the moment. However, holding the same fear or negative emotion toward someone day after day is blindly imitating oneself and one's past actions and capacities day after day. An inner act helps to bypass the fear and other possible negative emotions by allowing us the option of an inner act of service that does not require a physical interaction. We can pray for someone or offer an act of service for the progress of their soul. There are many indirect options.

There are also times when an outer act of service may not be appropriate. For example, 'Abdu'l-Bahá tells us not to **show** kindness to a liar. One can still shower that soul with unconditional love but we may judge it unwise to perform an outer act of service which would manifest that unconditional love. This is an extremely important concept because it clears up an apparent contradiction. There are innumerable passages in the writings of the Central Figures of the Faith exhorting us to love all humankind, but there are times when manifesting this love in the outer form would not be the wisest course of action. Notice below that 'Abdu'l-Bahá does not say 'Do not feel kindness'; He just says, 'Do not show it':

> Kindness cannot be **shown** the tyrant, the deceiver, or the thief, because, far from awakening them to the error of their ways, it maketh them to continue in their perversity as before.[10]

It is entirely our own decision whether an inner or outer act of service is more appropriate. A genuine act of service will help to heal strained relationships whether it is an outer or an inner act. The prime importance is that we do some act of service.

As the writings indicate, nothing can be stagnant in the world. Things either progress or regress. If we do not take a progressive action, we have, by default, committed to regression in the situation. So why not take the 'easy' way out by responding positively immediately, rather than waiting to acquire a bigger problem to address?

When we engage in acts of service, we become engaged in the process of investigating our own reality. Our reality is that of a servant of God. When we engage in an act of service, we uncover what kind of unique servant of God we are.

In the process we eradicate, bit by bit, the dust and veils of an illusionary identity formed by living in a culture immersed in blind imitation. We gradually eliminate from ourselves, and eventually from the wider society, every trace of blind imitation; and when we eradicate this, we eliminate the source of evil in the world. Thus the oneness of humankind, peace and all the divine promises can become manifest.

Investigating our own reality is necessary for the fullest release of our human potential. If we are not in touch with our own reality, we cannot investigate the reality of anything else, because illusion can only investigate illusion.

Being able to investigate reality (the first teaching of Bahá'u'lláh, according to 'Abdu'l-Bahá[11]) is true empowerment. This empowerment draws us closer to God, assists us to be more efficient and energetic, serene at our depths, to have better relationships – and the secondary benefits of knowing our true identity and having a way to learn from practice are limitless. Ultimately our capacities will increase, allowing us to find new solutions to our own and the world's problems.

Acts of Service as an Energy Source

Most of us have engaged in a line of work from which we have received compensation. An electrician comes to your house to fix a problem and is paid money in return. The electrician then takes the money and uses it for food, supplies or wherever he or she believes is the most urgent need. Any currency that we hold in our hand has circulated throughout the world by people who have all made similar choices. They are transferring money, a material commodity, for another commodity.

This concept empowers us to view acts of service as a potential energy source.

Rest assured, dear friends, that the hosts of the Abhá Kingdom stand ready to rush to the support of anyone who will arise to offer his or her acts of service to the unfolding, spiritual drama of these momentous days.[12]

Another spiritual concept is that we can pray and do good deeds for the progress of someone's soul in the next world. Indeed, our innate desire when someone has fallen ill is to pray for their recovery. This suggests that just as we transfer a material substance, like money, to where we need it on a day-to-day basis, perhaps we can take what we call the energy of divine assistance and transfer this force to where we think it is most needed in our lives.

We do think that the primary purpose of a genuine act of service is to draw the giver and receiver closer to God. We can have other material and spiritual motives for all our acts of service but having this deeper underlying primary purpose allows the energy of divine assistance to fill our soul so that we can then direct it with our God-given free will. As we see the beneficial effects of this power in our inner and outer lives, we will be encouraged to give and receive more and more acts of service. We will have created a virtuous cycle.

The two service questions, designed to help us engage with this cycle, began with an experience Ron had many years ago:

As a youth, I was serving on a committee that coordinated a ten-day session of the New York State Bahá'í Summer School. We had asked everyone we could think of to come and teach at our fledgling school and were shocked when Hand of the Cause Mr Zikrullah Khadem and his wife said yes.

It was an unbelievable experience. My head was in the clouds and my feet were left to fend for themselves the entire week. The funny thing is, I have no memory of what we talked about, only the spirit that pervaded those days. Mr Khadem made us laugh at the outset when he recalled that Shoghi Effendi had once told him that he would speak at places whose names he would never be able to pronounce. I still smile when I think of him trying to say 'Poughkeepsie', the city where the sessions were held.

At the end of the week, Mrs Khadem asked my friend Matthew Kurzius and me to drive her husband to Green Acre Bahá'í School in southern Maine, where he had his next speaking engagement.

She pulled me aside before we climbed into the car and told me that Mr Khadem was exhausted and recovering from heart trouble. Let him rest, she urged us, rather than tire him out by engaging him in conversation.

The six-hour trip proceeded in silence. Mr Khadem mostly slept, waking occasionally to tell us stories about Bahá'u'lláh. Matthew and I, obeying Mrs Khadem, said little.

About halfway, we stopped for lunch. Matthew and two others who were travelling with us ate at one booth and Mr Khadem and I shared another. As we did, a different side of him emerged. He was rested and in good spirits. We were about to order when he said, 'Ronnie, we both have to be careful of our health and watch our weight.' He told me about his recent heart trouble and then said, 'I ask you to eat only one hamburger.'

I replied, 'Mr Khadem, is it not true that the Bahá'í teachings encourage consultation?'

'Yes,' he responded, no doubt wondering where this was leading.

'Then I will compromise and order two hamburgers, no bread.'

He laughed so hard, I thought he might hurt himself. If there are such things as pearly gates, I imagine St Peter perusing his notebook when I eventually arrive and saying, 'Well, Ron, you have done a lot of silly things in your life. But you also gave a good laugh to a Hand of the Cause, so go on in. The all-you-can-eat buffet is waiting for you.'

We continued our drive north and arrived at Green Acre in the late afternoon. The enormous crowd gathered there seemed to swallow our precious passenger. Matthew and I stood on the porch and talked about where we would go to find some supper, since we'd arrived too late for the mealtime at Green Acre.

Just then, someone emerged from the crowd and put a hand on my shoulder and asked us to follow her. We entered the deserted dining room, where the only light was the late day sun shining through the window. We looked around and saw Mr Khadem sitting at a table alone with his untouched dinner in front of him. He had refused to eat until supper was also provided for the two boys that had brought him from New York. It was a simple act of kindness – an act of service but so powerful that the passage of time can never diminish its effect on my soul. At the time I thought that this must be what it was like to be in the presence of 'Abdu'l-Bahá. Of course, Mr Khadem, the soul and essence of self-effacement, would be horrified if he read this. I'll have to hope we don't read books in the next world.

The experience keeps teaching me new lessons, as well. The latest is the recognition that acts of service need to have a positive focus and be directed at the building up of the good in ourselves and others. Back at that restaurant, Mr Khadem hadn't made me feel bad or criticized me for being overweight. I knew his request about what I would order was offered as an act of service because everything he did was an act of service. The cumulative effect was a realization that I was being powerfully drawn towards the presence of 'Abdu'l-Bahá.

Diane also had an encounter with another soul that produced the same effect. She remembers:

In the summer of 1988 I was privileged to serve on the Green Acre Bahá'í School staff when Bahiyyih (given this name by 'Abdu'l-Bahá when she went on pilgrimage at the age of 12) Randall Winckler came to the school to conduct research for her father's biography. Her father, Harry Randall, had taken over the administration of Green Acre following the death of Sarah Jane Farmer, the school's founder.

I remember feeling terrified – intimidated – at the prospect of her arrival. But Bahiyyih was the essence of loving spirit to me. Not only did we work together but we had fun together. Her return to New England (the place of her birth) was her first after many years of living and serving in South Africa. She had a number of personal wishes for this visit and I was delighted to be asked to accompany her in the experience of many of them, including a walk on the beach, a bowl of clam chowder and her first visit to her father's grave in Massachusetts. The stories she shared about her pilgrimage to the Holy Land in the days of 'Abdu'l-Bahá kept me joyously spellbound.

But it was the way she counselled me about my own life's path that I remember most.

'No matter what talents you have been given in this world, it is only what you do for love of God that counts,' she said.

There was more detail but what stood out to me most was how I felt when she spoke. It was as though I were a speck of dust cradled and sheltered in the palm of a most loving hand. The idea was clear in my mind that this was as close to how it must have felt to be with

'Abdu'l-Bahá as anything I might ever know. It was the gift of an act of service, wrapped in empowering certitude. When I remember to remember it, all material obstacles diminish and detachment takes their place.

Diane also recalls her earliest introduction to the concept of service when, just after she had become a Bahá'í, she was elected to the Local Spiritual Assembly of Milwaukee, Wisconsin:

> Ardeshir Akhtar-Khavari, then in his eighties, moved into town and requested an appointment with the Spiritual Assembly to ask how he might serve it. He offered to give nine lessons on teaching in the manner of 'Abdu'l-Bahá, and also to share personal reminiscences from the 21 days he had spent living in the home of 'Abdu'l-Bahá when Ardeshir was 21. At each teaching session, one of Ardeshir's relatives would drive him and translate for him anything he might not understand into Persian/Farsi. Ardeshir had once had command of 11 languages but was finding that capacity slipping away.
>
> One day, no relatives were available and I was given the task of picking him up and 'translating', although I, of course, didn't speak a word of Farsi. This incident strengthened the heart connection I shared with this man who had been given the title of 'Conqueror of Arabia' by Shoghi Effendi, as he'd been the first Bahá'í to live in Mecca.
>
> I took to visiting him whenever I could where he lived alone in a retirement home. Because I experienced health challenges, occasionally I had a friend drive me and join in the visit.
>
> One day, Ardeshir said, 'It is so wonderful to see the two of you together. Of course, the driver benefits more, because she is providing the service, but both of you benefit. Every act of service enhances the unity of the entire community.'
>
> One day Ardeshir spoke at the Milwaukee Bahá'í Centre and asked, with a twinkle in his eyes, that he be given 19 per cent of the fruits of any of our efforts for his 'Abhá Kingdom account', Diane remembers.
>
> Thus 19 per cent of any service I have rendered in classes and this resulting book are clearly his, along with my deepest gratitude for his personal example in my life.

In terms of approaching a life of true purpose and service, our experience is that what can at first seem like a mechanical process becomes, after repeated practice, a completely natural way of relating to our fellow servants of God. A shift occurs from habitually acting from our lower nature to drawing upon our higher one, and before we know it, we have entered a new and better world – an eternal world.

Ron once asked Charlie Wragg, 'When does eternal life begin?'

He replied simply, 'When you begin to acquire what lasts forever.'

The next chapter explores our true identity as a servant of God who views life in terms of acts of service. This is our eternal identity and acts of service our eternal language. We want to acquire both.

SECTION TWO

All learning is sequential, although this concept is not always widely understood. No one would think it appropriate to attempt to teach a first-grader algebra when that child had not yet learned to add, subtract, divide and multiply – knowledge essential to mastering algebra. In such a child's shoes, we would likely feel frustrated, angry, depressed, with feelings of low self-esteem – even worthlessness. These feelings would inevitably be reflected in our behaviour too.

Multiply this problem by seven billion people and the magnitude of the problem is revealed. As human beings, our lack of learning and understanding about our true identity and purpose has reached a state of desperation indeed and is reflected in disastrous consequences at every level of human relationship. Dysfunctional, even deranged, behaviour includes the plethora of addictions and the damage they do, broken relationships and homes, and uncontrolled violence that erupts between two people trying to live together and nations trying to coexist. Such widespread dissolution and destruction affects all individuals, families and nations, whether poor or wealthy.

Best-seller lists brim with titles that promise a better life, yet life in our world seems to grow more 'desperate'. That word, chosen by the Universal House of Justice in that letter on human suffering written nearly 40 years ago, is, sadly, more accurate than ever.

In 1863 Bahá'u'lláh unveiled a Revelation that asserts that humanity is on the verge of a spiritual evolutionary leap into a future where lasting global peace is not only possible but inevitable. He described humanity as moving towards this stage of spiritual maturity through a dawning recognition of the oneness and interrelatedness in which it has been created, together with all of creation, and through the release of the gems of spiritual potential that await expression in every human heart.

Bahá'u'lláh's teachings assure us that as souls gain awareness and understanding of our truest identity and purpose, humanity will come to understand that the forces at work in human life are impelling us away from a centuries-old preoccupation with survival and 'fighting evil' towards our highest destiny: a creative, collaborative and potentially limitless building of the good, in which every individual has a part to play and every culture unique contributions to make.

In its 1974 letter the Universal House of Justice delineated in a sequential order the process by which such global transformation can occur. The members of the human family are invited to come to know and understand:

1) **Who they are**

2) **To what purpose they exist**

3) How they should act towards one another

4) Then they need to be helped to gradually apply these answers to everyday behaviour.

This next section will address the first two of these.

GENERAL IDENTITY AND INDIVIDUAL IDENTITY

The 'Who They Are' Question

True loss is for him whose days have been spent in utter ignorance of his self.[1]

It is not merely material well-being that people need. What they desperately need is to know how to live their lives – **they need to know who they are**, to what purpose they exist, and how they should act towards one another; and, once they know the answers to these questions they need to be helped to gradually apply these answers to everyday behaviour.[2]

1) **They need to know who they are.**

2) They need to know to what purpose they exist.

3) They need to know how they should act towards one another.

4) They need to be helped to gradually apply these answers to everyday behaviour.

No one can tell us who we are but each of us can unlock that inner door and see that what is within us truly is us. We all know how uncomfortable it feels when someone else tries to define who we are. Using a few practical tools we can each uncover the 'set of keys' that opens the door of our own heart.

In the past the investigation of reality of the individual was performed by designated leaders or man-made institutions that held power over the individual. Although society has advanced from this somewhat, an unavoidable remnant of that process has been the blind imitation of others that continues to be the source of the plethora of evils in the world.

The good news is that the days of sitting in a classroom or a pew and having someone investigate our reality for us are on the way out and will never come back. The Spirit breathed upon the world in this day has changed the collective consciousness of humankind.

The problem is that we are like a teenager caught between childhood and adulthood who knows in his heart that the time for independence has come but lacks the skills necessary to achieve that independence.

A person's knowledge of his identity and purpose develops through interactions that occur within the ever-evolving Covenant of God. The upcoming section on individual identity will provide examples of what is meant by this kind of interaction.

Humanity is now poised to make a giant leap forward in self-knowledge because it finally stands at the threshold of maturity that makes this possible. For the first time we have been deemed capable of receiving an indestructible, all-encompassing Covenant that includes an astounding wealth of sacred writings; an example, in the person of 'Abdu'l-Bahá, of how to actually live and embody such teachings; a Guardian of this worldwide endeavour, who created the structure of an administrative order that has diffused this spiritual wealth and healing throughout the world; and a divinely-directed, supreme governing body, the Universal House of Justice, that will guide humanity's spiritual progress in this new stage of development far into the future.

In revealing this new Covenant, Bahá'u'lláh described how it will create a new race of humankind and 'the Day that shall not be followed by night'.[3] As the Bible foretold so long ago, all things truly are made new.

Who among us hasn't felt desperate, at times, to know who we are and to what purpose we exist? In this very great day Bahá'u'lláh has invited us home to our own hearts to discover the answers that God has always treasured there.

A longtime friend of the authors, Larry Akeley, was someone who embodied the teaching of being 'unrestrained as the wind'[4] while walking the path of willing service that leads towards real happiness. He connected with others easily, very easily. Foremost in his mind, and his heart, was the desire to reflect to others who they truly are, because so often he could see in their faces that they had forgotten.

He would respond to people from his own inner perception of their true nature and purpose and he would frequently share with them a little card he'd designed that contained a quotation attributed to 'Alí from a book of two of Bahá'u'lláh's Tablets called *The Seven Valleys and the Four Valleys*. The card offered this question:

> Dost thou reckon thyself only a puny form
> When within thee the universe is folded?[5]

Author Jane Harper, in her book *The Universe Within: A Guide to the Purpose of Life*, describes how this question points us towards awareness of our capacity and powers:

> This is a very different perspective from how we generally define a human being or look at the course of our lives. We tend to look at life as if it were a sequence of events – some random, some inevitable – such as graduation from high school, a surgery, a summer vacation, the death of a loved one, a wedding, or an international trip. We often measure and describe our lives by our experiences or the goals we've achieved. Now, however, we can begin to understand that life is not merely a sequence of events but a process during which our highest potential develops.[6]

Those who received those little cards from Larry were grateful for an affirmation of an identity quite different from the one implied by the message they were receiving from a materialistic society. That message can leave us feeling like minute specks of dust in an infinite universe that offers our lives no lasting meaning. The message on Larry's card proclaimed the truth: that we are eternal spiritual beings that will long outlast the specks of dust that come and go in a material universe – and that we enfold a much greater kind of universe.

General Identity

God has revealed through the Bahá'í Revelation a torrent of knowledge about the human soul, a direct contrast to what was revealed before the coming of Bahá'u'lláh. In past dispensations, humanity had not acquired the capacity to understand the spiritual realms of God. Christ confirmed this fact when He stated:

> I have yet many things to say unto you, but ye cannot bear them now. Howbeit when he, the Spirit of truth, is come, he will guide you into all truth . . . (John 16: 12–13)

This is why the Manifestations of old spoke about the soul but did not explain its nature or reveal any of its mysteries. In the Qur'án, the holy book brought by Muhammad, the Prophet of Islam whose Revelation immediately preceded those of the Báb and Bahá'u'lláh, we can find this passage:

> They ask thee concerning the spirit. Say: the Spirit (was created) at the command of my Lord. But you have no knowledge given unto you except a little. (Q17:87)

In the Qur'án there are only a handful of statements about the nature of the soul whereas in the Bahá'í writings there are thousands of references to be found in the English translations alone. And that number will grow as more Tablets are translated in the future. However, this disparity is not a reflection on Muhammad or the Manifestations of the past.

This sudden explosion of knowledge has everything to do with humanity's emergence from immaturity and nothing to do with there being any difference in capacity between Bahá'u'lláh and the previous Manifestations of God. Each of the Manifestations had the capacity to reveal, as Christ described, 'all truth', but humanity had not yet the capacity to receive it.

We, too, want to avoid the mistake of trying to give what others are not ready to receive. Now, given the disparity between the truth that has been made available to us and the amount that humanity is actually encountering and applying, it isn't surprising that humankind's current perspective of the human reality is a mixture of truth, ignorance and distortions. And we certainly should not let this explosion of knowledge go to our heads because despite what we know, there is still more that we do not know about the human soul. The reality of the soul will always be a mystery.

Thou hast asked Me concerning the nature of the soul. Know, verily, that the soul is a sign of God, a heavenly gem whose reality the most learned of men hath failed to grasp, and whose mystery no mind, however acute, can ever hope to unravel.[7]

We can choose either to be frustrated when confronted with this mystery or enthralled with the prospect that through all the worlds of God we will continue to learn more about who we are. So, where do we begin in trying to answer the 'who they are' question, an answer that the Universal House of Justice has indicated we 'desperately need to know'?

According to 'Abdu'l-Bahá, existence consists of three conditions:

Know that the conditions of existence are limited to the conditions of servitude, of prophethood and of Deity . . .[8]

This is a very straightforward statement that is conveyed in several different ways in the Bahá'í writings. What it boils down to is that one can only be a servant of God, a Manifestation of God or God. A human being does not evolve to become a Manifestation and the Manifestation does not evolve to become God. It would follow, then, that if we are not consciously living in the condition of servitude, we are living in a world of illusion.

For example, Peter cannot become Christ. All that he can do is, in the condition of servitude, to attain endless perfections . . .[9]

Cling, O ye people of Bahá, to the cord of servitude unto God, the True One, for thereby your stations shall be made manifest, your names written and preserved, your ranks raised and your memory exalted in the Preserved Tablet. Beware lest the dwellers on earth hinder you from this glorious and exalted station.[10]

Deity

Prophethood

Servitude

'Abdu'l-Bahá's definition in *Some Answered Questions* that 'the conditions of existence are limited to the conditions of servitude, of prophethood and of Deity'[11] is represented in the symbol on rings that Bahá'ís often wear. Its image, in part, depicts these three conditions of existence.

This illustration is at once illuminating and extremely practical. We may often feel bewildered when we try to think of ourselves as souls because we're not quite sure what a soul does. However, when we equate our identity with that of a servant of God, then this identity implies acts of service that we need to give or receive on a daily basis. That is something we are capable of understanding.

'Abdu'l-Bahá eschewed all titles bestowed upon Him by Bahá'u'lláh except one: 'servant of God'.

> My name is 'Abdu'l-Bahá. My qualification is 'Abdu'l-Bahá. My reality is 'Abdu'l-Bahá. My praise is 'Abdu'l-Bahá. Thralldom to the Blessed Perfection is my glorious and refulgent diadem, and servitude to all the human race my perpetual religion . . . No name, no title, no mention, no commendation have I, nor will ever have, except 'Abdu'l-Bahá. This is my longing. This is my greatest yearning. This is my eternal life. This is my everlasting glory.[12]

We can all benefit from adopting our own personal version of how 'Abdu'l-Bahá describes His identity. For example, we might write:

> My name is _____(insert your name).

> I am a servant of God. I was born a servant of God. I will live eternally as a servant of God. I am not a writer, a plumber, a high school student, a husband, a wife, etc. I am a servant of God who writes books, fixes broken pipes, goes to school and is married.

Let all be set free from the multiple identities that were born of passion and desire, and in the oneness of their love for God find a new way of life.[13]

Thinking of our self as a servant of God helps to solve an ancient paradox. On one hand, we are created to know God, as the short obligatory prayer that Bahá'u'lláh has revealed reminds us each day ('I bear witness, O my God, that Thou hast created me to know Thee . . .'[14]), yet are also told repeatedly that God is unknowable. Since the Creator has chosen to form this bond with us, there must be, as in any relationship, some common ground. No common ground, no relationship. It is that common ground that we can gain knowledge of. The more we know about this relationship with God, the more we know about our own selves.

This is an important concept to grasp and it may seem a bit abstract when we are discussing a relationship with God. It might help to think about a relationship with someone we love. A few pages back, a quotation from Bahá'u'lláh indicated that our soul will always be a mystery. What this means in terms of relationships is that each of us is a mystery loving another mystery, which is made possible because of the understandable common ground that exists between any two people. That common ground has been created by cumulative acts of service – the giving and the receiving that has been exchanged between the two. This common ground – **this relationship** – is what we can know about.

It is also important to note that the genuine acts of service that we have exchanged with another person in this world form the eternal part of our relationship that transcends this material world. For example, the material gifts that we exchange with loved ones will return to dust but the love they were given with will last forever.

What is the connection between relationships and the concept of investigating our own reality? The fact is that personal investigation of one's reality is an abstract endeavour and it can be difficult to assess progress. However, the more successful we are in uncovering our true self, the better the decisions we will make regarding our lives and the people in them, which translates into healthier and happier relationships. This will provide us with tangible evidence that we are making progress on the path of servitude and self-discovery.

For the purposes of this book, we are calling the phrase 'servant of God' the general identity of a human being. This phrase symbolizes the state of consciousness that is present the moment an individual realizes and accepts that she or he is a servant of God.

The question then becomes: Once we know our general identity, how do we make progress in developing our unique, individual identity?

Individual Identity

One obstacle that prevents us from discovering and developing our unique individual identity is the human tendency to fall into the trap of imitating someone else's life and behaviour rather than living one's own life.

As Bahá'u'lláh stated in *The Seven Valleys*:

> In their search, they have stoutly girded up the loins of service, and seek at every moment to journey from the plane of heedlessness into the realm of being. No bond shall hold them back, and no counsel shall deter them.
>
> It is incumbent on these servants that they cleanse the heart – which is the wellspring of divine treasures – from every marking, and that they turn away from **imitation**, which is following the traces of their forefathers and sires . . .[15]

In this instance, it is not only what Bahá'u'lláh says that is significant but also where He shares it. This quotation is at the very beginning of The Seven Valleys, the Valley of Search. This is a clear statement at the outset that the obstacle that prevents us from proceeding on the journey through the seven valleys from the 'plane of heedlessness to the realm of being' is imitation.

Here we see an important connection between imitation, the investigation of reality and the process of discovering our unique individual identity. We know that the underlying cause of evil in the world is imitation or blind imitation. We know that, according to 'Abdu'l-Bahá, it is only through the investigation of reality conducted by each individual for himself or herself that we can eradicate imitation, and thus evil, from the world. And now, this further guidance from Bahá'u'lláh reveals that imitation can actually prevent us from the discovery of our unique individual reality.

The journey that begins with the awareness of being a servant of

God – our general identity – takes place on the path of servitude and leads to our unique individual identity.

General Identity→→→→→→→→→→→Unique Individual Identity
A   Path of Servitude   B

Within this journey, the process of self-discovery is related to nearness to God.

> The duty of the people of Bahá is to tread the path of servitude to the Divine Threshold, spread God's Teachings, and establish a spiritual civilization.[16]

In his book *The Covenant of Bahá'u'lláh*, Adib Taherzadeh states that the only station befitting a human being is servitude. 'To the extent that the individual believer abides on the plane of servitude, he will grow closer to God and become the recipient of His power, grace and bounties.'[17]

> If the travellers seek after the goal of the Intended One (*maqṣúd*), this station appertaineth to the self – but that self which is 'The Self of God standing within Him with laws'.
> . . . Although at the beginning, this plane is the realm of conflict, yet it endeth in attainment to the throne of splendour.[18]

In order to commit to any significant journey, we must have a great desire and be highly attracted to the destination. It requires true resolve to traverse 'the realm of conflict' on the path of servitude (surrendering to the spiritual nature – what is of God – rather than to the lower nature, concerned only with survival) and approach the 'Divine Threshold' and 'the Self of God standing within Him with laws'.

What if that seeking after the 'Intended One' results in the neverending discovery of the true unique self? The seeking takes place within the eternal, evolving Covenant of God, and thus our identity ('that self which is "The Self of God standing within Him with laws"') becomes moulded and shaped by living within this Covenant.

Although this is a mystical journey, the actual steps are simple and practical, as in the oft-quoted phrase that Dr David Starr Jordan, President of Leland Stanford Junior University, used in his introduction of

'Abdu'l-Bahá: "'Abdu'l-Bahá will surely unite the East and the West: for He treads the mystic way with practical feet.'[19]

'Abdu'l-Bahá has also described three elements of transformation – 'knowledge, volition and action'.[20]

The measurement of the third element, action, can be assessed in the two service questions:

1) At this moment in time, what is the act of service I am capable of giving that the other person is capable of receiving?

2) At this moment in time, what is the act of service I am capable of receiving that the other person is capable of giving?

In order to be effective, acts of service must be generated in conscious awareness that we are a servant of God. Powerful stresses are created if there is a disconnection between what we believe to be our identity and the purpose behind our actions. Powerful stresses are also created if we are not allowed to enact our own, unique acts of service. To live to our highest potential, it seems that we need to come into consciousness of our true selves and also to establish a balance between our being and our doing that is rooted in our truest purpose.

Ideally, acts of service flow naturally from the heart of a servant of God to humanity. This is what produces constant measurable growth. Lest we be carried away by any unrealistic and unhelpful delusions of grandeur, we can remember that no matter how far we progress, we always remain in the condition of servitude.

When we give or receive acts of service that are consistent with the Covenant of God, we become engaged in the process of investigating our own reality and gradually reveal who we really are. In that process, we gradually disperse the dust and veils of an illusory identity formed by living in a culture immersed in blind imitation, and discover our true and unique individual identity.

The process begins with a genuine act of service that is always motivated by the attributes of God that are latent within each of our hearts and await our free-will decision to bring out those 'gems of inestimable value'.[21] How we choose to show love, receive forgiveness, etc. in an act of service is our own spiritual fingerprint, and just like our physical fingerprint, it is unique to us.

Nobody in the past, present or future will love exactly the same way that each of us does. Each time that we give or receive, an attribute of God – a facet of the infinite jewel – is revealed. In this way we make an invaluable contribution because we have added to what can be perceived of divinity. And because we are all capable of making such a contribution, this means that each individual is absolutely indispensable.

Think of how incomplete a puzzle feels if just one piece is missing. It is only when we see our fellow servants of God as unique and indispensable that we can truly relate with them as servants of God. When we rise above conflicting personalities, we can see with the eye of oneness, as asked of us by Bahá'u'lláh.

> The essence of all that We have revealed for thee is Justice, is for man to free himself from idle fancy and imitation, discern with the eye of oneness His glorious handiwork . . .[22]

This guidance was reiterated by the Universal House of Justice in its Riḍván 2008 message:

> Only if you perceive honour and nobility in every human being – this independent of wealth or poverty – will you be able to champion the cause of justice.[23]

'Abdu'l-Bahá wrote:

> O Company of God! To each created thing, the Ancient Sovereignty hath portioned out its own perfection, its particular virtue and special excellence, so that each in its degree may become a symbol denoting the sublimity of the true Educator of humankind, and that each, even as a crystalline mirror, may tell of the grace and splendour of the Sun of Truth.[24]

We need to look deeper than someone's surface personality, which often does not seem to mesh with our own, and truly see our fellow servants of God. Each soul has been given a particular virtue and special excellence, a unique gift that leads us to the giver of that gift: the Sun of Truth, the Manifestation of God.

The authors often find that as we observe and appreciate the acts of service of others, we discover that these make visible another soul's uniqueness and indispensability.

Ron recalls:

My mother was a Bahá'í and a chiropractor in the 1950s when both were considered 'cults' and she thus encountered strong opposition to these from friends and family. But rather than becoming bitter or weakened by this, she was a joyful, effective teacher of both her health philosophy and her religion.

She was also the most compassionate person I have ever met, a compassion inspired by her great love for 'Abdu'l-Bahá. She took seriously His counsel to 'be like me' and the poor in her midst were, indeed, her trust.

Over the 44 years that she practised, she became less formal. Her white uniforms turned into house dresses and her structured 15-minute appointments became free-flowing events that might last two hours. When she was in her seventies, her practice dwindled along with her energy and she worked mainly for the love of the work and the opportunity to share love and spirit with others.

'Dr Mary', as everyone called her, had a special gift working with sick children. Adults were sometimes intimidated by her strong personality but that was not what the little kids ever saw.

One day I came to her house after work and found my now 80 year old mother and my 11 year old daughter cleaning my daughter's old bike – not out in the backyard but in my mother's waiting room. They were having a grand time, laughing and making a mess.

When I asked what they were doing, my mother promptly replied, 'We're cleaning up this bike for Linda (not her real name).'

Linda, a girl about my daughter's age, had a terminal illness. Once a week her father carried Linda to my mother's office. No one had any illusions about a cure but my mother was able to take away a lot of her pain.

I was puzzled by my mother's plan to give this bike to Linda and said, 'Mom, you know Linda will never ride that bike.'

She replied, 'Of course I know that but Linda believes she will and that is all that matters.'

All kinds of people, young and old, came to believe all kinds of things around my mother. Linda believed she could dream about tomorrow and I came to believe that my mother was unique and indispensable.

Diane remembers how deeply blessed she felt to have become a Bahá'í in Milwaukee, Wisconsin, in the 1980s:

It was a great privilege and exciting start to join a large, extremely diverse community with a Bahá'í centre in a transitional neighbourhood on the edge of the inner city. The number of treasured souls I met and who assisted my development defies my ability to express my gratitude.

Among them were a couple, Hedwig and Spark Hashimoto. They were among the senior members of the community and I was grateful they decided to 'adopt' me. A childless couple, they assisted any number of their nephews, cousins and exchange students from Japan to successfully handle life in this world while they ardently shared the healing message of the Bahá'í Faith with everyone they met. They maintained a very humble profile within the Bahá'í community yet were always engaged in active service.

The list of measures they took to help me personally and befriend me would fill a volume of its own. All they asked in return was to be remembered after they departed this world because they had no children to remember them. The remembrance I share here is a tiny part of the great debt I owe them.

The single event I remember most was when I was scheduled for gall bladder surgery. Hedy arranged for people to pray for me around the clock for 24 hours on the day of the surgery. I didn't know this until later but I was profoundly aware of being cradled in the most loving hands throughout that day.

A few days later a friend came to visit me. She told me that Hedy was in the car in the parking lot waiting for her to return because she wanted me to have visitors but felt she did not have the appropriate clothing to wear to visit me. The devoted humility and active service of the Hashimotos serves as an ongoing example to me all my days.

Phyllis describes one childhood experience that continues to help her monitor her words and actions:

My best friend's father, Al Shaw, was kind, soft-spoken, gently humorous and thoughtful. A hard-working man with a big family, he always made time to interact with his kids and their friends, whether drawing caricatures of us as we watched, giggling, or hunkering down his tall frame to help us construct the miniature villages that took over his living room floor. Whenever he spoke with me, as he always made time to do, I felt as though I truly mattered.

One day, this kind man gave me a real gift, though it felt like something quite different at the time. I was riding in the back seat of his wood-panelled station wagon after he'd picked up a small gang of us from a Girl Scout Christmas party. We were all comparing the gifts we'd drawn in the gift exchange and I wasn't very happy with mine.

When one of my peers leaned over and observed under her breath that someone had obviously spent the low end of the price range for it, I felt licence to begin holding forth on how worthless and disappointing it was and how unfair that I got it. I was probably enjoying my companions' attention as I bewailed my plight and began berating both the gift and the giver.

I'll never forget the look in that dad's eyes as they met mine in the rear view mirror and he said evenly but firmly, 'Hey now, that's *enough.*'

I'd never heard this man raise his voice, and he didn't this time – just set an unambiguous and important limit. Although I wanted to disappear in disgrace at that moment, I've been as grateful to him for this as I have for the hundreds of kindnesses he's bestowed on me.

Knowing that he was disappointed and displeased with my behaviour had an enormous impact on me. He didn't need to point out things like how potentially hurtful what I was saying was, how the donor of that gift could have been sitting in the car, for all I knew. Awareness of all of this came very quickly once I was jolted out of my self-focused tirade.

All he had to tell me, this man whose opinion I cared about so much and who I knew cared about me, was that it was time to stop, with four words that changed my life forever. He intervened with an act of true service, while helping me set for myself a limit that has somehow become internally reinforcing.

He was the first to bring to my attention what Bahá'u'lláh emphasizes about the power of what we say:

Every word is endowed with a spirit, therefore the speaker or expounder should carefully deliver his words at the appropriate time and place, for the impression which each word maketh is clearly evident and perceptible.[25]

'Abdu'l-Bahá encouraged us to

Turn all your thoughts toward bringing joy to hearts.[26]

A welcome remedy for the kinds of thoughts that often weary our hearts is to instead contemplate examples of how individuals offer acts of service that help others discover important answers to the 'who they are' question. This is a very purposeful kind of 'building of the good' that can have great effect and also assist us to focus on our highest reality, rather than on those discouragingly worldly things that, like fighting evil, can take up such an inordinate amount of our energy and attention.

Doing this will also lead our hearts to many wondrously uplifting joys and mysteries. For in the latest chapter of God's Revelation that has blessed the world today, a new Covenant has unveiled elements of reality and spiritual purpose that the world has not seen before.

Meaning and the Covenant of Bahá'u'lláh

If there is one word that encapsulates the desperate need of humanity described in detail in the 1974 letter of the Universal House of Justice on material suffering, that word is 'meaning'. We are desperate to know what our lives are all about. Yes, we want to know the overall reason for the existence of humanity but we really want to know why we, ourselves, have been created as individuals.

The illustration below could easily have the words 'love' or 'justice' inside the inner circle instead of 'servant of God'. Every atom, every individual, eventually discovers the meaning of its unique existence within the Covenant of God. As we shall read, our meaning is revealed when we serve the Covenant:

Today, the Lord of Hosts is the defender of the Covenant, the forces of the Kingdom protect it, **heavenly souls tender their services**, and heavenly angels promulgate and spread it broadcast. If it is considered with insight, it will be seen that all the forces of the universe, in the last analysis serve the Covenant.[27]

This illustration of the station of a 'servant of God' surrounded by and immersed in the Covenant conveys another critical concept: meaning is found within that Covenant, and nowhere else.

The phrase 'servant of God' could be merely the 'murmur of syllables and sounds'[28] that might mean anything outside the Covenant of Bahá'u'lláh because there is no infallible context. As we write this, the Bahá'ís of Iran are undergoing a fresh wave of persecution at the hands of those who proudly call themselves servants of God. And countless others are being similarly persecuted by those who believe themselves to be such servants.

The Covenant provides the context and the structure where meaning is found, and this includes our true identity. This has not changed as revelation from God has unfolded throughout time. What has changed is the capacity of humanity to receive, understand and apply divine knowledge, which has evolved as the Covenant of God has evolved.

In the Tablet of Salmán[29] Bahá'u'lláh explains an unnoticed mystery in the Qur'án regarding the statement of faith that is the foundation of Islam: 'There is no God but Him'. Bahá'u'lláh describes the word 'no' as 'the letter of negation', which precedes the affirmation 'but Him' in the phrase, and explains that thus, in the past, those who violated the Cause of God dominated over the faithful.[30] Thus, like the followers of all the religions of the past, humanity at the time of Muhammad did not possess the maturity to prevent their religion from developing schisms and divisions and splintering into sects.

Bahá'u'lláh goes on to say that the letter of negation has now been removed and has been replaced by the phrase 'He is God' and that this latest evolution of the Covenant of God will not devolve into countless warring sects.[31] Humankind is now capable of keeping its part of the Covenant of God and not dividing the religion. At the same time that we have been given the opportunity to investigate reality for ourselves, we have also, for the first time, been given a personification of meaning in the personal example and the words of 'Abdu'l-Bahá, the Centre of the Covenant:

> As to the most great characteristic of the revelation of Bahá'u'lláh, a specific teaching not given by any of the Prophets of the past: It is the ordination and appointment of the Centre of the Covenant.[32]

Such an unbreakable, intricately complex Covenant makes possible the answering of the 'who they are' question, as well as the other questions in the 1974 letter of the Universal House of Justice on material suffering. It is now possible to discover our unique individual identity and unique individual purpose to a degree that was not previously possible in human history.

How this happens in practical terms is that as we interact with some element of this vast Covenant, such as the example of 'Abdu'l-Bahá, a fragment of sacred writings or a law of God, this interaction generates inspiration that is eventually translated into a genuine act of service. Our motivation is most likely one of improving our relationships with our fellow servants of God but something far deeper transpires, which may, initially, go unnoticed. We are bringing out from the latent state of potentiality our true self and purpose.

Let's look again at this quotation:

> If the travellers seek after the goal of the Intended One (*maqṣúd*), this station appertaineth to the self – but that self which is 'The Self of God standing within Him with laws'.[33]

This process of generating genuine acts of service leads to our deeper awareness of our spiritual nature and the discovery of our true self, rather than the resistance or insistence of the ego self which is motivated by a lower-nature focus on survival.

Proceeding from the point of knowing our general identity to discovering our unique individual identity is the most exciting and fulfilling journey of self-discovery we can undertake. And because we are eternal spiritual beings, it is an eternal journey.

As our spiritual nature flourishes through the giving and receiving of acts of service (two aspects of one reality, much as inhalation and exhalation are in breathing), so these acts of service are generated when our truest identity interacts with the elements of the Covenant of God.

* * *

At the end of each chapter we offer a brief reminder about some essential aspects of an act of service, which empowers us to investigate our own reality and come to see with our own eyes. The goal in adding these facets to our Options Chart is to help us employ the two service questions even more effectively.

The Options Chart

Facet to be considered in determining an act of service	Optional	Not Optional	Chapter
Act must be generated by a servant of God		X	5
Act must be in conformity with the Covenant		X	5

The whole, completed Options Chart can be found in appendix 1.

6

'TO WHAT PURPOSE THEY EXIST'

The Key that Frees Us

The Purpose of the one true God, exalted be His glory, in revealing Himself unto men is to lay bare those gems that lie hidden within the mine of their true and inmost selves.[1]

'What is the purpose of our lives?'
'Abdu'l-Bahá: 'To acquire virtues.'[2]

In this chapter, we seek to answer the second question in the implied sequence of what we must know about ourselves.

1) They need to know who they are.

2) **They need to know to what purpose they exist.**

3) They need to know how they should act towards one another.

4) They need to be helped to gradually apply these answers to everyday behaviour.

It is not merely material well-being that people need. What they desperately need is to know how to live their lives – they need to know who they are, **to what purpose they exist**, and how they should act towards one another; and, once they know the answers to these questions they need to be helped to gradually apply these answers to everyday behaviour.[3]

Why Purpose is So Important

The importance of the concept of purpose has its roots in the writings of Bahá'u'lláh. In previous dispensations humanity was required to believe and obey. Now, in this latest enfoldment of God's Covenant with man, Bahá'u'lláh says:

> Observe My commandments, for the love of My beauty.[4]

'Observe My commandments, **for the love of My Beauty**', for a purpose that is so very attractive and engaging for the soul. Among several meanings, 'observe' means 'abide by' or 'keep', and here Bahá'u'lláh exhorts us to do this not out of fear or apprehension but out of love. We can choose a variety of material and spiritual purposes in our lives as long as they are compatible with this primary purpose to know and love God.

Again, Bahá'u'lláh links our created purpose with love:

> Having created the world and all that liveth and moveth therein, He, through the direct operation of His unconstrained and sovereign Will, chose to confer upon man the unique distinction and capacity **to know Him and to love Him** – a capacity that must needs be regarded as the generating impulse and the primary purpose underlying the whole of creation.[5]

The question then becomes: How do we fulfil our primary purpose to know and love God? We suggest the key is found in this Hidden Word:

> O Son of Spirit! I created thee rich, why dost thou bring thyself down to poverty? Noble I made thee, wherewith dost thou abase thyself? Out of the essence of **knowledge** I gave thee being, why seekest thou enlightenment from anyone beside Me? Out of the clay of **love** I moulded thee, how dost thou busy thyself with another? Turn thy sight unto thyself, that thou mayest find Me standing within thee, mighty, powerful and self-subsisting.[6]

We are asked to turn our sight inward. And what would we see? We would see that we are made from the knowledge and love of God.

Therefore this is where our focus is best directed and what we can benefit from striving to see in everyone else.

Granted it is easier to see the image of God in some people than in others but that simply means that we need to put forth greater effort to see what we absolutely know exists in every human being, whether or not it is visible to us.

Again, as always, 'Abdu'l-Bahá offers an example:

> He 'saw the Face of His Heavenly Father in every face' and reverenced the soul behind it.[7]

And if we see the Face of our Beloved in every face, how can we do anything else but serve that person by offering our purest and most selfless acts of service?

The bar has been raised to a higher level in this new era, as Bahá'u'lláh explains in this Hidden Word:

> O Children of Adam! Holy words and pure and goodly deeds ascend unto the heaven of celestial glory. Strive that your deeds may be cleansed from the dust of self and hypocrisy and find favour at the court of glory; for ere long the assayers of mankind shall, in the holy presence of the Adored one, **accept naught but absolute virtue and deeds of stainless purity**. This is the day-star of wisdom and of divine mystery that has shone above the horizon of the divine will. Blessed are they that turn thereunto.[8]

This Hidden Word cites 'absolute virtue' and 'stainless purity' as the necessary purpose – or some could say intention or motive – behind the deed. We are told that the 'assayers of mankind' will accept nothing less. It's impossible to overestimate the value of 'deeds of stainless purity' and, obviously, such deeds are ones that arise from a willing, responsive heart.

> By My life! All that are on earth shall pass away, while good deeds alone shall endure.[9]

Here is where the two service questions prove especially valuable as a means by which we may assess the choice we will make in each moment:

1) **At this moment in time**, what is the act of service I am **capable** of giving that the other person is capable of receiving?

2) **At this moment in time**, what is the act of service I am **capable** of receiving that the other person is capable of giving?

Just as we must decide what act of service we are capable of 'at this moment', we must also ask what purpose we are capable of 'at this moment'. To reach the heights that Bahá'u'lláh invites us to attain, our deeds must rise from the dust of self-interest to the heaven of 'deeds of stainless purity'.

This means that when we ask ourselves what deed or act of service we are capable of giving or receiving, the component of purpose must be a part of the question. Indeed, the purpose motivating why we give or receive will bring clarity about what would be the most effective act of service. It will also infuse the act of service itself with the spiritual power that is rooted in truthfulness.

We aspire to make our purpose as pure as possible but it is never helpful to fall into negativity when we fall short. The truth is, we will always fall short of perfection. There will always be more moments, more tomorrows. Growth is slow, when you consider that we are eternal spiritual beings.

The following story illustrates the capacity of a pure, selfless act of service to carry enormous spiritual power.

At the second Bahá'í World Congress, held in 1992 to celebrate the centenary of Bahá'u'lláh's passing, Rúḥíyyih Khánum shared stories about some early Bahá'ís she had known whose deeds had inspired her. Marion Jack, or 'Jackie' to her friends, was a fellow Canadian whom she dearly loved. Marion was known to be quite ageless, was happy in the company of young and old alike and made friends wherever she went. Around 1930, in the latter part of her life, a life that had been devoted to a path of service, Marion moved to Sofia, Bulgaria, in order to offer service and was still there on the eve of World War II. Her Bahá'í friends, including Rúḥíyyih Khánum, pleaded with her to leave, saying that at the age of 73, and with a heart condition, she probably could not survive the imminent invasion by the Nazis. Even Shoghi Effendi, the Guardian of the Bahá'í Faith, implored her to leave, although he stopped short of telling her to do so. She begged him to let her stay at her post, to 'remain

64

at the switch'[10] and do what she could to help, and he finally relented.

Marion Jack was struggling on a meagre pension when a bombing raid destroyed the hotel in which she was living. Fortunately, she was in another part of the city during the raid but she had nothing left except the clothes on her back. She was taken to a school in the country along with other Canadians who had been caught in the conflict. It was wintertime, her bed was a cot and her 'room' was an unheated hallway. Her friends received no further information about her until after the war; an international aid worker finally brought Rúḥíyyih Khánum a letter from Marion, who wanted everyone to know that she was all right.

Rúḥíyyih Khánum wrote back immediately, asking what Marion needed. As Rúḥíyyih Khánum shared this story with her audience at the World Congress in New York nearly 50 years later, she told the thousands gathered there that she and Shoghi Effendi would have done anything, supplied Marion with anything she asked for.

Finally a reply came. Inside the envelope were two sheets of paper. One was a tracing of the outline of Marion's feet. The other was a note that asked politely whether she might be sent a pair of shoes.

Marion Jack didn't ask for money or a train or plane ticket – or a life of well-deserved comfort many might think she had earned. With so much to rebuild in war-torn lives, Marion still chose to stay in Bulgaria and to serve. Her selfless life of service was epitomized in those two pieces of paper. She passed away in Bulgaria in 1954, having, indeed, remained at her post to the end. Her purpose was pure service to humanity and God, and the purity of that service ensured that she would be forever revered as an immortal heroine of the Faith.

We are all capable of doing so much more than we think or imagine because within each of us lies a gift placed there by God, a gift that is made visible through our unique acts of service.

Marion Jack was neither wealthy nor exceptionally gifted in worldly terms but she will always be remembered for the nature of her devotion and her faithfulness to the commitments she had made.

The Role of Purpose in Overcoming Blind Imitation

Within a wide range of fields from arts to business, a process known as conceptual thinking has begun to appear. Sometimes called out-of-the-box thinking, it is generally defined as the ability to identify patterns or connections between situations that are not obviously related, and to identify key or underlying issues in complex situations. It includes using creative, conceptual or inductive reasoning.

Confirmation for this line of reasoning, and the difference between fact-based and concept-based thinking, can be found in Book 6 in the sequence of courses of the Ruhi Institute, entitled *Teaching the Cause*:

> . . . is teaching the same as giving out information? Consider, for example, the fact, most central to Bahá'í belief, that Bahá'u'lláh is the Manifestation of God for today. The statement 'Bahá'ís believe that Bahá'u'lláh is the Manifestation of God for today' by itself is only an **item of information [a fact]** . . . Yet, is the mere pronouncement of this fact sufficient to help most people recognize the Station of Bahá'u'lláh?
>
> Now consider something which, though related to this fact is not simply information, namely, the **concept** that 'Bahá'u'lláh is the Manifestation of God for today'. While a piece of information needs only to be given and received, absorbing a concept involves understanding.[11]

A concept 'involves understanding'. We cannot be content to merely repeat over and over again a litany of facts and call that teaching. That is blind imitation.

Now let us hear from a highly skilled practitioner of conceptual thinking:

> Should prayer take the form of action?
>
> *'Abdu'l-Bahá*: Yes: In the Bahá'í Cause arts, sciences and all crafts are (counted as) worship. The man who makes a piece of notepaper to the best of his ability, conscientiously, concentrating all his forces on perfecting it, is giving praise to God. Briefly, all effort and exertion put forth by man from the fullness of his heart is worship, **if it is prompted by the highest motives and the will to do service to humanity**. This is worship: to serve mankind and to minister to the needs of the people. Service is prayer. A physician ministering to the sick, gently, tenderly, free from prejudice and believing in the solidarity of the human race, he is giving praise.[12]

Conceptual thinking is 'the ability to identify patterns or connections between situations that are not obviously related'. If we look again at how 'Abdu'l-Bahá defines prayer and worship, we find that seemingly unrelated acts such as making a piece of notepaper or a physician ministering to the sick are given the exalted status of prayer and worship if – and it is a significant qualifier – 'it is prompted by the highest motives and the will to do service to humanity'.

This brings us back to purpose, which is one of the fundamental common denominators or connecting threads between realities that do not seem to be connected. 'Abdu'l-Bahá is saying that everything an individual does during a typical day can be a prayer or an act of worship if motivated by the purpose of pure service to humanity.

Contrast this expansive view of reality with the tunnel vision of blind imitation, which might insist that prayer can only be called prayer if the individual performs an unvarying set of rituals. It is easy to see how blind imitation 'stunts the mind', which, in turn, precludes the investigation of reality and the possibility of discovering new ideas.

Conceptual thinking, when it occurs in a mind animated by the spirit of faith (we'll discuss this important animating power further in a later chapter), results in an explosion of creativity that leads to unending advances in the arts and sciences. And, in the process, it helps to eliminate blind imitation.

Conceptual thinking is the natural thought process of the spiritual nature, the result of which is then translated into acts of service.

But beyond solving business problems or creating new art forms, conceptual thinking enables us to perceive the underlying interconnectedness of all reality until all that is seen is an all-encompassing oneness motivated by a common **purpose** that is inherent in all life forms: to draw closer to what has created us.

He looketh on all things with the eye of oneness, and seeth the brilliant rays of the divine sun shining from the dawning-point of Essence alike on all created things, and the lights of singleness reflected over all creation.[13]

An exploration of the connection between conceptual thinking, purpose and the spiritual nature, and how they all work together to thwart blind imitation will continue in chapter 9 on the mind and chapter 10 on the spiritual nature.

For now, an experience of Ron's can help illustrate the interrelation of these elements in a concrete way. His first job was working in a factory where he literally did the same work day in and day out. Time seemed to stand still and he thought he would lose his mind. If ever there was a situation that lent itself to blind imitation, this was it, and there are millions of people whose work life is similar.

Then Ron came to realize that although he had no control over what he did outwardly on a daily basis, he had total freedom over his inner life, because he could choose the **why or for what purpose** he did the work. He could choose from an unlimited number of divine purposes, even choosing a different purpose each day. Those choices could only be made by asking the inner questions of his own self and answering in accordance with what attributes he felt needed to be increased in his life. One day, his purpose could be concentrating on doing a task as precisely as possible, for example, and the next could involve seeking to show kindness in all of his interactions.

This helped him keep sight of his primary purpose and identity, as he reminded himself that he was a servant of God and that his overall purpose was to serve God and humanity. Although outwardly it might appear as though he were doing the same thing every day, inwardly he was choosing from an unlimited number of options and approaching his living and working (and worshipping) consciously, leaving blind imitation no chance to take control of his thinking or actions.

'To What Purpose They Exist'

In the previous chapter we attempted to answer the 'who they are' question posed by the Universal House of Justice. We focused on 'Abdu'l-Bahá's living model of what it means to be a servant of God. His was not a secluded existence removed from the ills that afflict humanity. If someone was hungry, He fed him. If someone was sick, He would provide the healing attention she needed and if someone had no clothes, He was known to give him the garment He was wearing.

A study of 'Abdu'l-Bahá's life reveals that His identity, purpose and everyday behaviour blended together in a seamless harmony that defined His faith – 'servitude to all the human race (is) my perpetual religion'.[14]

With 'Abdu'l-Bahá as example, how might our own life demonstrate a harmonious oneness between our identity, our purpose and our faith? Perhaps some of the unhealthy stresses that create inner turmoil and cause problems in our relationships will fade away if we are successful in answering this question and achieving this goal.

The Inseparable Relationship Between 'Who They Are' (Identity) and 'To What Purpose They Exist' (Purpose)

The following demonstrates how any attempt to separate our identity or reality from purpose results in a complete loss of meaning. Marian Lippitt, an early mentor to the authors, stressed the importance of this connection in an illustrative story she often told.

Imagine an isolated backwoods community barely touched by civilization. An appliance delivery truck takes a wrong turn and ends up lost on the area's mountain roads. A family is sitting on the porch of its log cabin when the truck rolls by on the bumpy dirt road. A modern refrigerator tumbles unnoticed from the back of the truck and lands upright on the road, much to the family's amazement. They encircle the gleaming white contraption and try to figure out what it is and how they could use it. They finally decide to put it on the front porch and use it to store their muddy boots.

The question is: What is it? A mechanical device to keep food cold, as its creator intended, or a boot storage-locker, because of the current purpose this family has assigned to it? What is humorous when the subject is refrigerators and muddy boots becomes tragic when it involves human beings who are unaware of their God-given identity and purpose. Not only do we suffer because we don't know our true identity and purpose, but everyone we interact with suffers as well.

Our primary purpose must be consistent with our identity as a servant of God. This purpose is designed to strengthen that identity, and if we lose track of it, we also lose our way, drifting from one illusionary identity to another.

We suspect that such a disconnection from our true identity and purpose is the cause, at the deepest level, of the tremendous anxiety and stress we encounter in the world. Picture yourself standing with your arms outstretched, attached to ropes that are pulling you in opposite directions. That's what a soul can feel like when it experiences a conflicted sense of purpose, rather than being grounded within – and liberated by – its truest purpose.

There is an inseparable connection between purpose and reality, and now it becomes clear why the Universal House of Justice connects humanity's ignorance of its true identity and purpose with widespread material suffering. Those who don't know 'who they are' or 'to what purpose they exist' are ill-equipped to make wise decisions. Decisions based on the illusions of the material world rather than spiritual truth and reality result in negative consequences in every aspect of the individual's material, intellectual and spiritual life, which often results in material, intellectual and spiritual suffering.

Basically, spiritual beings cannot live successful lives motivated solely by material purposes, and any attempt to do so results in failed relationships and dysfunctional behaviour. This may not be apparent in individual lives but it becomes obvious as the social order grows more complex and is crippled by poverty, disease, wars, genocide and the destruction of the environment.

A passage in a letter written by the Universal House of Justice makes a connection between knowing the purpose of life and creating a better world:

> All over the world tremendous efforts are being made to improve the lot of mankind – or of parts of mankind, but most of these efforts are frustrated by the conflicts of aims, by corruption of the morals of those involved, by mistrust, or by fear. There is no lack of material resources in the world if they are properly used. **The problem is the education of human beings in the ultimate and most important purpose of life and in how to weld the differences of opinion and outlook into a united constructive effort.**[15]

The problem that seems to continually thwart 'a united constructive effort' in our inner life, the circle of our family and friends, our communities or the world at large is that this stage of our eternal journey takes place in a material world, with its material requirements. So how do we avoid what seems to be an unavoidable clash between the material and spiritual aspects of life? 'Abdu'l-Bahá suggests a remedy:

> O thou son of the Kingdom! All things are beneficial if **joined** with the love of God; and without His love all things are harmful, and act as a veil between man and the Lord of the Kingdom. When His love

is there, every bitterness turneth sweet, and every bounty ren, dereth a wholesome pleasure.[16]

The key word in the above is 'joined', as 'Abdu'l-Bahá says. 'Joined with the love of God.' He does not advocate living the detached life of the cloistered ascetic. Rather, in such assertions as 'Work done in the spirit of service is worship'[17] He urges individuals to create a beneficial harmony in all aspects of their material and spiritual life. He explained that joining the spiritual with the material in our lives is the key to a successful, balanced life.

When we go to work, provide food and shelter for our family or pay our taxes, we are urged to do so motivated by the love of God. That way we join a material purpose with a spiritual one. If we find that we're incapable of joining a spiritual purpose to a material one, then perhaps we need to question whatever it is we are doing in the material world. It may be we aren't capable, at this moment, of a particular act of service, but it also could mean that the material act itself is not the best investment of our time or is even a hindrance to our spiritual life.

Joining material and spiritual purposes acts as a check-and-balance mechanism for our life in this world, so that we neither become an ascetic nor a materialist. The best vehicle for this 'joining' is the path of service.

Another practical by-product of this kind of growth through service is that it helps to eliminate any unhealthy material attachments we may have acquired, together with the unhealthy fear that always accompanies them. (An exercise in appendix 5, 'The Guiding Light of the Fear of God', is designed to help assist in this process.)

As for what 'Abdu'l-Bahá meant by 'joined with the love of God', we envision the love of God as a big umbrella that encompasses all divine purposes and attributes of God. We include a few here but the list is endless because when the Word of God is read with an eye towards identifying the purpose statements it contains, they begin to appear constantly.

The following are just two examples of joining a spiritual purpose with a material one and we each benefit when we make our own list.

Spiritual Purpose	Material Purpose
The sign of love is . . . patience under My trials.[18]	Living with chronic illness.

Now, on some days, the 'joining' of two purposes like these might work for us, while on other days it won't. We don't need to be rigid about this, nor fall into the habit of blindly imitating what we did yesterday. In every moment we change and the situation changes. The spiritual purpose of acquiring the virtue of radiant acquiescence might serve us better today than on a different day. It is important to keep asking ourselves the inner questions about just what effect a marriage of spiritual and material purposes will have in our lives.

Spiritual Purpose	Material Purpose
To show love to one another, 'cooperate and mingle in accord'.[19]	Going to work, doing my job, participating with others in devotion or learning.

Again, our attempt might be successful today but tomorrow we might have a difficult day at work and all we're capable of that day is to 'bear and endure' and, perhaps, try to acknowledge and appreciate the gifts and blessings in our lives.

After we define some twin purposes of our own, the important thing is to reflect on how to join a spiritual purpose with a material one. As we do this, divine guidance is a crucial part of the process. (Appendix 2 offers a list of some divine purposes that have been revealed to us.)

It benefits us to develop the skill of reading the sacred writings with an eye towards finding the purpose statements that they contain. As we do, we'll discover that in the face of the overwhelming mystery that is an inseparable part of our being, knowing our purpose in any given situation is what allows us to focus our energy where it will do the most good.

O Thou Whose tests are a healing medicine to such as are nigh unto Thee . . .[20]

In this phrase from a prayer, 'Thou' is God, the greatest mystery of all; 'to such' is the individual who is also described in the writings as a mystery. We cannot know why God chooses to send us a particular test on a particular day in our life – another mystery. We do know that God intends the test to be 'a healing medicine' for us.

When we know what our purpose is, then it becomes easier to focus our minds on where it would be best for us to focus our attention.

One result is that we ask better questions. Instead of, 'God, are you sure that this is the test I need at this time for my personal healing?' we ask, 'God, help me to understand and accept that the **purpose** of this test is "healing medicine" for me.'

Thinking in terms of purpose helps us to choose the most productive path of action and prevents us from wasting precious time and energy in unhealthy fear or negativity. In the face of overwhelming mystery, we can know that the best course of action is an act of service that can draw us closer or 'nigh unto' God.

The following quotation not only identifies some purpose statements but also applies these to our own life. Our first challenge is not to let these words simply remain on the page but to take them personally. In this quotation the word 'you' has been replaced with a blank that we can fill in with our name and make God's purpose for humanity our very own purpose.

Verily, God has chosen _____ for His love and knowledge; God has chosen _____ for the worthy service of unifying mankind; God has chosen _____ for the **purpose of investigating reality** and promulgating international peace; God has chosen _____ for the progress and development of humanity, for spreading and proclaiming true education, for the expression of love toward your fellow creatures and the removal of prejudice; God has chosen _____ to blend together human hearts and give light to the world.[21]

The question then becomes, how can each of us, personally, choose 'to blend together human hearts'[22] or carry forward 'an ever-advancing civilization'?[23]

Purpose: The Key that Frees Us from the Prison of Self

When asked how He survived so many years of harsh physical imprisonment, 'Abdu'l-Bahá made an astounding statement:

> There is no prison but the prison of self . . .[24]

He went on to say:

> . . . I was happy all that time in prison. When one is released from the prison of self, that is indeed release, for that is the greater prison. When this release takes place, then one cannot be outwardly imprisoned.[25]

He was never in prison because He never assumed the false identity of a prisoner. His identity/purpose was not dependent on where He slept at night or whether there were bars on the windows. He was a servant of God who continually served God by serving His fellow servants. That's who He was before, during and after He was in prison.

Why is this information practical? We may not suffer imprisonment like 'Abdu'l-Bahá but at some point in our life we will find ourselves in circumstances that sure feel like prison. Maybe there was a time that we were stuck in a job that we hated but, owing to various circumstances, could not leave. For others, it might be a situation in school, a personal relationship or a serious illness.

If we let material circumstances define our identity and purpose, then we place our consciousness in the prison of the material world, which, as 'Abdu'l-Bahá has described, is the source of all misery:

> If we suffer it is the outcome of material things, and all the trials and troubles come from this world of illusion.[26]

Furthermore, He says:

> . . . all our sorrow, pain, shame and grief are born in the world of matter; whereas the spiritual Kingdom never causes sadness. **A man living with his thoughts in this Kingdom knows perpetual joy.** The ills all flesh is heir to do not pass him by, but they only touch the surface of his life, the depths are calm and serene.[27]

We highlighted 'A man living with his thoughts in this Kingdom knows perpetual joy' but is it really that simple? Just sit in the backyard and sip a glass of cool lemonade while reminding ourselves that we are servants of God, and our purpose is to serve God? Oh, if only it were that easy.

> Thoughts may be divided into two classes:
> (1st) Thought that belongs to the world of thought alone.
> (2nd) Thought that expresses itself in action.
> Some men and women glory in their exalted thoughts, but if these thoughts never reach the plane of action they remain useless: the power of thought is dependent on its manifestation in deeds. [28]

This guidance brings us back to the importance of the two service questions. It is needful that we both maintain a consciousness of our true identity/purpose and express it in acts of service.

Maybe we aren't able to maintain that state of consciousness for decades, as 'Abdu'l-Bahá did, but even a moment, a minute or a whole precious hour of living with our thoughts 'in the Kingdom' and knowing 'perpetual joy' is something wonderful. If we were dying of thirst, would we only accept an endless supply of water from a mountain stream or would we be grateful for a small cupful?

Purpose as a Magnet for Divine Assistance

Suppose an individual could throw a ball the length of a football field. This would be a powerful demonstration of transference of energy. But what if it were possible to throw it to the moon? That would be transference of energy incredible beyond belief.

What if it could not only be thrown clear out of this world but that degree of energy was also readily available to better our own life and the lives of others?

'Abdu'l-Bahá says:

> The progress of man's spirit in the divine world, after the severance of its connection with the body of dust, is through the bounty and grace of the Lord alone, or through the intercession and the sincere prayers of other human souls, or through the charities and important good works which are performed in its name.[29]

75

That is, someone can perform an act of service for another soul **not even in this world** and that soul makes 'progress'. This is an astounding statement. Have we realized that we are capable of such a powerful act of service? And yet how many times have we all felt inconsequential and insignificant? How often have we seen ourselves as a 'puny form' when, in reality, 'the universe is folded up' within us?[30]

And what if, in return for our act of service, we were given divine assistance that we could use to help even more people, realize our own dreams and become more creative? Might not this be suggested in the following passage?

> It is known and clear that today the unseen divine assistance encompasseth those who deliver the Message.[31]

> Teach ye the Cause of God, O people of Bahá, for God hath prescribed unto every one the duty of proclaiming His Message, and regardeth it as the **most meritorious of all deeds**.[32]

Thus when we share the Message of God in our being and in our doing – something which is defined as the most meritorious of all deeds – we receive divine assistance. What if we envision such assistance as a form of energy, perhaps the highest form of energy that exists? What if this energy, this grace, is a resource upon which we can draw on an 'at this moment' basis, as needed, in order to contribute to the 'building of the good' in our own life and the lives of others?

A few pages ago we learned how 'Abdu'l-Bahá expanded the meaning of prayer and worship. He gave great value to everyday acts and said they could rise to the level of worship if motivated by love for and service to humanity.

The essence of sharing what is of God is an act of service motivated by the purpose of drawing nearer to God, and encouraging and supporting others as they do the same. How might this become the motivating purpose behind every single interaction we have with our fellow servants of God? How might every act become, potentially, such an exchange of divine light, thereby bestowing on both giver and receiver the subsequent energy of divine assistance?

With the free will we have been given, such assistance is ours to use as we choose. This energy could be used to improve our health, the well-being of someone else, or could be employed to help us become ever more effective and creative in the ways that we pursue our path of service. 'Abdu'l-Bahá has described:

> I now assure thee, O servant of God, that, if thy mind become empty and pure from every mention and thought and thy heart attracted wholly to the Kingdom of God, forget all else besides God and come in communion with the Spirit of God, then the Holy Spirit will assist thee with a power which will enable thee to penetrate all things, and a Dazzling Spark which enlightens all sides, a Brilliant Flame in the zenith of the heavens, will teach thee that which thou dost not know of the facts of the universe and of the divine doctrine. **Verily, I say unto thee, every soul which ariseth today to guide others to the path of safety and infuse in them the Spirit of Life, the Holy Spirit will inspire that soul with evidences, proofs and facts and the lights will shine upon it from the Kingdom of God.**[33]

We are promised that if we arise to carry out a divinely bestowed purpose – to infuse the Spirit of Life and accompany others on such a path, in such a process – we will, assisted by the dazzling spark of the Holy Spirit, be taught what we do not yet know of the facts of the universe and other divine mysteries. Thus if we wish some mystery to be revealed to us, whether within our work and creative efforts or elsewhere on our path, the energy of divine assistance can be used for this purpose. The possibilities, it would seem, are without end or limit, as long as we are in concert with the conditions 'Abdu'l-Bahá specifies:

- our mind become empty and pure from every mention and thought

- our heart become attracted wholly to the Kingdom of God

- we forget all else besides God, and

- we come in communion with the Spirit of God.

Might we attempt this for just one moment? Because that's all it takes to have this experience: just one moment that can take us far beyond any limitations that our mind and lower natures may perceive about time or space.

How Purpose Can Improve the Quality of Our Lives Forever

Purpose is the means by which we can concentrate all our powers and faculties to achieve a goal. Its life-changing power is now a widely-accepted concept described in countless schools of thought and best-selling books.

But as with any kind of power, it is how we use it that determines its highest worth. In the 1974 Universal House of Justice letter on material suffering, there is additional guidance that relates to the concept of purpose. As it explores its central theme of material suffering, the letter goes on to say:

> We should also remember that most people have no clear concept of the sort of world they wish to build, nor how to go about building it. Even those who are concerned to improve conditions are therefore reduced to combatting every apparent evil that takes their attention. Willingness to fight against evils, whether in the form of conditions or embodied in evil men, has thus become for most people the touchstone by which they judge a person's moral worth. Bahá'ís, on the other hand, know the goal they are working towards and know what they must do, step by step, to attain it. **Their whole energy is directed towards the building of the good, a good which has such a positive strength that in the face of it the multitude of evils – which are in essence negative – will fade away and be no more. To enter into the quixotic tournament of demolishing one by one the evils in the world is, to a Bahá'í, a vain waste of time and effort.** His whole life is directed towards proclaiming the Message of Bahá'u'lláh, reviving the spiritual life of his fellowmen, uniting them in a divinely created World Order, and then, as the Order grows in strength and influence, he will see the power of that Message transforming the whole human society and progressively solving the problems and removing the injustices which have so long bedevilled the world.[34]

In light of this guidance, does it not make sense that our acts of service be motivated by the purpose of a 'building of the good'?

The following story, which describes a real event, is an example of the kind of 'positive strength' the Universal House of Justice says it is possible to demonstrate when confronted by evil.

In 1994 the Green family was vacationing in Italy. They were touring the countryside in a rented car when criminals mistook their car for that of a rival drug gang and sprayed it with gunfire. Miraculously, the mother and father were unharmed but their seven year old son, Nicholas, had been shot in the head. For two days he lingered in the hospital until he was pronounced brain dead.

Italians were horrified and filled with shame that this should happen to a visitor to their country and they expected a torrent of condemnation. Instead, the couple donated their child's organs to seven gravely ill people in that country and the Italian people were shocked even further. At that time it was uncommon for Italians to donate their organs, but as a result of this incredible act of service, the rate of organ donation has quadrupled in Italy since that time, a rate of increase no other country has experienced, according to the website of the Nicholas Green Foundation.[35]

Nicholas's parents returned to Italy the following year and were honoured in a national ceremony where they were welcomed by the seven recipients of the organ donations. These included two teenagers who had been given the gift of sight. (The full story is told in the book of the father, Reg Green, *The Nicholas Effect*.)

Motivated by a noble purpose, the couple had acted towards the building of the good when they might have lashed out in anger, despair or grief – all very understandable human responses. And consequently, the spirit of their response has reverberated in many lives.

Purpose is a necessary component of a spiritual life. Our spiritual nature knows that the 'why' or purpose behind our actions is often the determining factor as to what constitutes a spiritual act.

A Suggested Exercise – Using Purpose to Focus the Power of Prayer

Step One: Clear your mind of distractions using whatever approach or meditation tools you prefer. Silence is likely a part of this, or quieting music. Take all the time you need to do this; it is well worth that time.

Step Two: Wait, with willing trust, and see which person or people may come into your awareness.

Step Three: Choose a prayer or inspirational passage – perhaps see which one you are somehow drawn towards and let its wisdom and illumination connect with one of those individuals who have come to your mind.

Step Four: After you have read this prayer or passage, remain silent again for a while. Listen for how the wisdom you've imbibed might relate to, or suggest an act of service you might offer to, this individual, whether outwardly or inwardly. Here, it is also helpful to express your gratitude for guidance and for the assistance that can help you carry out such an act with a pure heart and clear purpose, motivated only by love for what is of God.

This is a deceptively simple exercise that can powerfully assist us to internalize what divine guidance is offering to us and translate that wisdom into acts of service. It is also a way to bring new meaning to devotional and meditative time, and to avoid the trap of blind imitation, even in this.

* * *

Let's recap what we have learned in this chapter by adding facets to our Options Chart.

Facet to be considered in determining an act of service	Optional	Not Optional	Chapter
Acts must come from the application of an attribute of God/virtue		X	6
Acts must be motivated by the pure love of God OR have a divine purpose OR have a human purpose linked with a divine purpose		X	6
We choose the specific purpose or virtue	X		6

The whole, completed Options Chart can be found in appendix 1.

SECTION THREE

This section includes the chapters 'The Spirit of Faith: Power Source for Investigating Reality'; 'Using the Faculty of Inner Vision'; and 'Servant to Truth: The Mind Animated by the Spirit of Faith'.

We make no attempt in this book to provide an exhaustive explanation of such concepts as spirit, soul, mind and the nature of the individual. Our focus is to offer some simple, practical tools that we hope will help with the individual's investigation of reality – knowledge that can then be applied to figure out how we should 'act towards one another' and improve our 'everyday behaviour'.

The first two of these chapters address powers of our higher, or spiritual, nature. The third describes how, when these powers are activated and employed, the mind can fulfil its highest purpose, as servant to truth, by truly investigating reality rather than blindly imitating the past, whether in outward actions or inner beliefs.

The knowledge and discoveries that we encounter and uncover in that investigative process can, through the willingness that arises from our heart, be directed into divinely-inspired (and informed) acts of service.

These acts – knowledge in motion through willing action on a path of service – empower and enable us to answer the third question posed by the Universal House of Justice:

1) They need to know who they are.

2) They need to know to what purpose they exist.

3) **They need to know how they should act towards one another.**

81

4) They need to be helped to gradually apply these answers to everyday behaviour.

7

THE SPIRIT OF FAITH

Power Source for Investigating Reality

The spirit of faith is crucial to the investigation of our reality because it provides the animating power that makes possible the level of perception required to investigate the spiritual component of any reality, including our own. We will explain more about the animating power of the different degrees of spirit that are derived from the Holy Spirit in the next three chapters.

As we approach the prospect of 'how we should live our lives', it is the spirit of faith animating our spiritual nature that alone possesses the capacity to respond to this question. Trying to answer it with anything less will inevitably result in blindly imitating the past because we will be operating only from the limited premise of what we think we know, rather than from the kind of knowledge and inspiration to which the spirit of faith can gain access. Thus we'll see no new or beneficial result.

Here is how 'Abdu'l-Bahá explains the spirit of faith:

> The fourth degree of spirit is the heavenly spirit; it is the spirit of faith and the bounty of God; it comes from the breath of the Holy Spirit, and by the divine power it becomes the cause of eternal life. It is the **power** which makes the earthly man heavenly, and the imperfect man perfect. It makes the impure to be pure, the silent eloquent; it purifies and sanctifies those made captive by carnal desires; it makes the ignorant wise.[1]

The following is a list of what 'Abdu'l-Bahá has indicated this incredible divine power makes possible in our life:

1) The spirit of faith is the cause of eternal life.

2) The spirit of faith makes the earthly man heavenly.

3) The spirit of faith makes the imperfect man perfect.

4) The spirit of faith makes the impure to be pure.

5) The spirit of faith makes the silent eloquent.

6 The spirit of faith purifies and sanctifies those made captive by carnal desires.

7) The spirit of faith makes the ignorant wise.

Let's contrast what 'Abdu'l-Bahá says about what the spirit of faith with what He says about the human spirit:

> This [human] spirit has the power of discovery; it encompasses all things. All these wonderful signs, these scientific discoveries, great enterprises and important historical events which you know are due to it. From the realm of the invisible and hidden, through spiritual power, it brought them to the plane of the visible.[2]

We see that the power of the human spirit enables us to uncover the 'scientific discoveries' of the material world, whereas the spirit of faith, this aspect of our higher, spiritual nature, empowers us to discover the mysteries of the spiritual world, of which we, too, within the spirit of faith, are a part.

> . . . the spirit of faith which is **of the Kingdom** consists of the all-comprehending grace and the perfect attainment and the power of sanctity and the divine effulgence from the Sun of Truth on luminous light-seeking essences from the presence of the divine Unity. And by this Spirit is the life of the spirit of man, when it is fortified thereby, as Christ saith: 'That which is born of the Spirit is Spirit.' And this Spirit hath both restitution and return, inasmuch as it consists of the Light of God and the unconditioned grace.[3]

Thus the spirit of faith itself is 'of the Kingdom' and 'consists of the

Light of God and the unconditioned grace'. All souls are animated by the human spirit and, according to 'Abdu'l-Bahá, 'the mind is the power of the human spirit'.[4]

The following quotation also makes it clear that unless the human spirit and its power, the mind, are aided by the spirit of faith, the individual cannot understand spiritual realities.

> But the human spirit, unless assisted by the spirit of faith, does not become acquainted with the **divine secrets** and **heavenly realities**.[5]

It is absolutely necessary to be animated by the spirit of faith in order to investigate our reality because we and everyone we interact with are a 'divine secret' and a 'heavenly' reality. According to 'Abdu'l-Bahá, we are not fully alive without the power of the spirit of faith:

> Now these 'spirits' are not reckoned as Spirit in the terminology of the Scriptures and the usage of the people of the Truth, inasmuch as the laws governing them are as the laws which govern all phenomenal being in respect to generation, corruption, production, change and reversion, as is clearly indicated in the Gospel where it says: 'Let the dead bury their dead' . . . inasmuch as he who would bury these dead was alive with the vegetative, animal and **rational human soul**, yet did Christ – to whom be glory! – declare such dead and devoid of life, in that this person was devoid of the **spirit of faith**, which is of the Kingdom of God.[6]

Now we can understand why 'Abdu'l-Bahá says that the spirit of faith is 'the cause of eternal life'. Yes, life continues in the next world but as 'Abdu'l-Bahá explains in *Some Answered Questions*, life without the spirit of faith, in relative terms, is the life of a 'stone'.[7]

For our practical objectives in this world, the spirit of faith is crucial because it awakens our eternal spiritual nature, which is what we need to answer those four crucial questions.

It is in the realm of human relationships, where we try to figure out 'how they should act towards one another', that the presence or absence of the spirit of faith is felt, and it isn't that difficult to determine the truth. If our spiritual nature animated by the spirit of faith is guiding our life, then our instinctual reaction is discovering the act of service that 'builds up the good' in our relationships. The acts of service flow naturally from our conscious identity as a servant of God. There is no anguish about what to do, only an awareness of a deep inner process to determine the outer form of the desire to serve one another.

It is very important not to feel discouraged if we are not able to achieve this state of being every second of the day. It is important to know that this state of being is the ultimate goal, and to know when we are succeeding or failing in attaining it. Helpful focus for doing this is provided by the two service questions because they are actually requests that our spiritual nature take control of our life and relationships.

Indeed, it isn't possible to effectively use the two service questions without being animated by the spirit of faith because the choices for our acts of service are restricted to that portion of reality that we perceive. Without the spirit of faith augmenting the power of the mind, our acts of service would be limited to meeting the material needs of ourselves and others. We would be able to see that someone was thirsty for a glass of water but unable to see that they were thirsty for the love of God, the mercy of God and all the other 'virtues of the Kingdom'.

When we wish to offer that gift that quenches the deepest spiritual thirst, the healing remedy that can even unite the world, the spirit of faith is at play both in our own actions and within the soul with whom we interact. When offering this gift it's important to bear in mind that this exchange is sacred business. It is not taking place in the thought world but from heart to heart, and those hearts are what the love of God, out of which we were all created, has claimed for itself.

O Son of Being! Thy heart is My home; sanctify it for My descent. Thy spirit is My place of revelation; cleanse it for My manifestation.[8]

Thus while we are striving to connect with human hearts in a spirit of love and service, and listening to another as carefully as we are able, it is the spirit of faith within ourselves, and our ability and willingness to hear its voice from another's heart, that enables us to share this most precious of gifts in a way that will assist the recipient to receive it.

The spirit of faith helps us remember the mystery of all the unseen assistance involved with such an act of service, as we continue to ask ourselves:

1) At this moment in time, what is the act of service I am capable
    of giving that the other person is capable of receiving?

2) At this moment in time, what is the act of service I am capable
    of receiving that the other person is capable of giving?

In its guidance, the Universal House of Justice has asked that we
perform 'progressively more complex and demanding acts of service'.[9]
For an example of how the spirit of faith affects all our acts of service,
'Abdu'l-Bahá explains that it is through the power of the spirit of faith
that we can be conscious of the fact that we are eternal spiritual beings.
Someone who knows this to be true will place far more importance
on the eternal divine attribute behind giving someone a glass of water
than on the material act itself. A hundred years from now it won't really
matter that we brought someone a glass of water but a million years
from now it will still matter that we offered this act of service with love
in our heart.

The glass, the water and our bodies will all be gone. The attributes of
God that we use to inspire our acts of service become eternal qualities
of our soul and of the soul of humanity. Our acts alter the condition of
humanity forever.

How does the spirit of faith contribute to answering the 'how we
should live our lives' question? Eternal spiritual beings have absolutely
no fear that their acts of service – whether of giving or of receiving –
will be rejected because they know that this is a spiritual impossibility.
Do we think of ourselves and others as souls that have been created to
seek light, the attributes of God? Certainly, a proffered glass of water
can be rejected but the essence of the act of service, the love or kindness
or generosity motivating it, has a life-changing effect on the giver and
the receiver.

Why does the receiver also benefit? Because each eternal spiritual
being has been created to accept and embrace the eternal spiritual
attributes of God, in whatever way they may come. Knowing this to be
true, a soul with its focus on the spiritual reality lives with far less fear.

Basically, the spirit of faith enhances immeasurably both our perception and the quality of the choices we make based on such enhanced
perception. Ultimately, this enhanced perception made possible by the
spirit of faith results in wise choices that then become translated into

complex acts of service. We also realize a deepening awareness of our own reality, which contributes to the fostering of strong and spiritually-based relationships.

How We Come into Contact with the Spirit of Faith

Bahá'u'lláh has described the means by which we come into contact with what is of God within our own selves:

> These energies with which the Day Star of Divine bounty and Source of heavenly guidance hath endowed the reality of man lie, however, latent within him, even as the flame is hidden within the candle and the rays of light are potentially present in the lamp. The radiance of these energies may be obscured by worldly desires even as the light of the sun can be concealed beneath the dust and dross which cover the mirror. Neither the candle nor the lamp can be lighted through their own unaided efforts, nor can it ever be possible for the mirror to free itself from its dross. It is clear and evident that until a fire is kindled the lamp will never be ignited, and unless the dross is blotted out from the face of the mirror it can never represent the image of the sun nor reflect its light and glory.
>
> . . . He hath ordained that in every age and dispensation a pure and stainless Soul be made manifest in the kingdoms of earth and heaven . . . These Essences of Detachment, these resplendent Realities are the channels of God's all-pervasive grace. Led by the light of unfailing guidance, and invested with supreme sovereignty, They are commissioned to use the inspiration of Their words, the effusions of Their infallible grace and the sanctifying breeze of Their Revelation for the cleansing of every longing heart and receptive spirit from the dross and dust of earthly cares and limitations. Then, and only then, will the Trust of God, latent in the reality of man, emerge, as resplendent as the rising Orb of Divine Revelation, from behind the veil of concealment, and implant the ensign of its revealed glory upon the summits of men's hearts.
>
> From the foregoing passages and allusions it hath been made indubitably clear that in the kingdoms of earth and heaven there must needs be manifested a Being, an Essence Who shall act as a Manifestation and Vehicle for the transmission of the grace of the Divinity Itself,

the Sovereign Lord of all. Through the Teachings of this Day Star of Truth every man will advance and develop until he attaineth the station at which he can manifest all the potential forces with which his inmost true self hath been endowed. It is for this very purpose that in every age and dispensation the Prophets of God and His chosen Ones have appeared amongst men, and have evinced such power as is born of God and such might as only the Eternal can reveal.[10]

Author Adib Taherzadeh has described how the spirit of faith begins to shine its light in the life of our soul.[11] By turning to the Manifestation of God and receiving the outpourings of the Manifestation's glory, the soul becomes illumined with the spirit of faith:

> The highest station destined for man is to be illumined by the 'spirit of faith', which comes through recognition of the Manifestation of God for the age and through obedience to His commandments. To attain this station is the very purpose for which God created man.[12]

The soul needs to recognize and establish this spiritual link, as in this age, the main purpose of the Revelation of Bahá'u'lláh is to illumine the human soul, endow it with the spirit of faith and thereby bring into being a new creation of humankind, one that embodies the highest purpose for which it has been created, capable of coming together in unity.

Such an enlightened soul is fully capable of answering question number three: **They need to know how they should act towards one another.**

When we come into contact with this aspect of our highest reality, the spirit of faith, the elevated level of perception that it offers not only enables us to see problems clearly and how to solve them but also enables us to perceive more opportunities and possibilities available to us and how to make best use of them. Without this kind of vision, we remain trapped in the prison of imitating the past, what we think we know and what we perceive to be limits imposed upon us.

Taking steps of action on a path of service seems to be another way of deepening our connection with, and living from, the spirit of faith. And doesn't it seem logical that if we lead a life of willing, believing servitude, we will be imbued with more and more of the spirit of faith?

How We Lose Touch with the Spirit of Faith

The simple answer is by being attached to this world instead of being attracted towards what is of God. In *The Revelation of Bahá'u'lláh*, Adib Taherzadeh goes on to explain: 'Because of its attachment to this world, the soul is not always illumined with the "spirit of faith".'[13]

In one of His Tablets, Bahá'u'lláh, addressing His followers, has likened the soul to a bird:

> Ye are even as the bird which soareth, with the full force of its mighty wings and with complete and joyous confidence, through the immensity of the heavens, until, impelled to satisfy its hunger, it turneth longingly to the water and clay of the earth below it, and, having been entrapped in the mesh of its desire, findeth itself impotent to resume its flight to the realms whence it came. Powerless to shake off the burden weighing on its sullied wings, that bird, hitherto an inmate of the heavens, is now forced to seek a dwelling-place upon the dust.[14]

It is possible, of course, to free up the 'sullied wings' that we will necessarily acquire as an inevitable result of living in this world. But like an unlit candle, we cannot bring this about on our own. This is where prayer, meditation, fasting, reflection and service – all those spiritual essentials prescribed from age to age – help us to remember and reconnect with the nobility of our true spiritual identity. And it is, in the end, the spirit of faith, and the willingness to acknowledge and submit to it, that prompts us to reach for these as the remedies that we know will bring that effect.

The spirit of faith is the power source of the spiritual nature – indeed, of our very being – and is responsible for the highest level of perception available to a human being. The spiritual nature has the ability to create complex acts of service, the very essence of 'how they should act towards one another'.

In the next chapter we will explore the process by which we ask the inner questions that result in genuine acts of service.

Now, we'll add the facets we have identified in this chapter to our Options Chart:

The Options Chart

Facet to be considered in determining an act of service	Optional	Not Optional	Chapter
Animated by the spirit of faith – person seeking scientific answer	X		7
Animated by the spirit of faith – person seeking spiritual answer		X	7

The whole, completed Options Chart can be found in appendix 1.

USING THE FACULTY OF INNER VISION

The favours of God are all-surrounding, but should the conscious eye of the soul of man remain veiled and darkened, he will be led to deny these universal signs and remain deprived of these manifestations of divine bounty. Therefore, we must endeavour with heart and soul in order that the veil covering the eye of **inner** vision may be removed, that we may behold the manifestations of the signs of God, discern His mysterious graces and realize that material blessings as compared with spiritual bounties are as nothing.[1]

Therefore, we must thank God that He has created for us both material blessings and spiritual bestowals. He has given us material gifts and spiritual graces, outer sight to view the lights of the sun and **inner vision** by which we may perceive the glory of God.[2]

While this chapter includes information that may be applied in a wide variety of ways, including as a means of drawing out our hidden gifts and talents, its main purpose is to focus on the role of the faculty of inner vision in addressing the following questions posed by the Universal House of Justice:

1) They need to know who they are.

2) They need to know to what purpose they exist.

3) **They need to know how they should act towards one another.**

4) They need to be helped to gradually apply these answers to everyday behaviour.

In this chapter we will learn more about how to use the inner faculties we possess in order to investigate our own reality. We will also discover that the inner faculties are essential in trying to figure out how we 'should act towards one another'. It is only logical that if we used only our outer faculties, we would be relating only to the outer material aspects of our fellow servants of God, which is not sufficient to answer the questions posed by the Universal House of Justice.

> **The soul has two main faculties**. (a) As outer circumstances are com-
> municated to the soul by the eyes, ears, and brain of a man, so does
> the soul communicate its desires and purposes through the brain to the
> hands and tongue of the physical body, thereby expressing itself. The
> spirit in the soul is the very essence of life. (b) The second faculty of
> the soul expresses itself in the world of vision, where the soul inhabited
> by the spirit has its being, and functions without the help of the mate-
> rial bodily senses. There, in the realm of vision, the soul sees without
> the help of the physical eye, hears without the aid of the physical ear,
> and travels without dependence upon physical motion. It is, therefore,
> clear that the spirit in the soul of man can function through the physi-
> cal body by using the organs of the ordinary senses, and that it is able
> also to live and act without their aid in the world of vision. This proves
> without a doubt the superiority of the soul of man over his body, the
> superiority of spirit over matter.[3]

This quotation explains how 'the soul expresses itself in the world of vision' but the Bahá'í writings also mention the spiritual counterpart of other physical senses, such as inner hearing and inner tongue, and allude to a spiritual counterpart to the sense of smell.

> . . . he would inhale, at a distance of a thousand leagues, the fragrance
> of God . . .[4]

Think of inner vision as a kind of shorthand for all our spiritual senses. Inner vision, or the more familiar term 'intuition', refers to the inner powers of the soul. There are numerous quotations in the Bahá'í writings that describe the material world as a reflection of the spiritual world.

'The Celestial Universe is so formed that the under world reflects the upper world.' That is to say whatever exists in heaven is reflected in this phenomenal world.[5]

. . . the outward is the expression of the inward; the earth is the mirror of the Kingdom; the material world corresponds to the spiritual world.[6]

This concept enables us to understand spiritual laws because we already have the experience of living with physical laws every day. Likewise, the concept that we have spiritual senses that correspond to physical senses is also something we can comprehend.

We can imagine conversations in the near future between scholars of the material world and the scholars of the spiritual world that will go something like this: 'I have observed this phenomenon in the material world. What do you think the counterpart would be in the spiritual world?' Or, 'I think I have had this spiritual experience. I wonder where I can find its counterpart in the material world?'

This chapter offers an outline of the practical steps required in order to efficiently use our inner faculties but, first, it is helpful to look at an example that demonstrates the limitations of our outer faculties.

The book *Inner Knowing* by Helen Palmer profiles the lives of world-famous scientists, with an emphasis on their moment of discovery. In each case the individual experienced a tremendous leap in knowledge, powered by the faculty of inner vision or intuition, which resulted in discoveries that changed the world.

One such scientific explorer was Nobel Prize recipient Melvin Calvin, who was trying to find a missing compound in the process of photosynthesis. There was no book or person that could provide the answer. But one day, while he was sitting in his car waiting for his wife, a complete vision appeared in his mind that answered all his questions. In those 30 seconds he essentially encompassed the idea that would award him the Nobel Prize for Chemistry.

Let's revisit a passage from 'Abdu'l-Bahá that explains how this is possible:

I now assure thee, O servant of God, that, if thy mind become empty and pure from every mention and thought and thy heart attracted wholly to the Kingdom of God, forget all else besides God and come in communion with the Spirit of God, then the Holy Spirit will assist thee with a power which will enable thee to penetrate all things, and a Dazzling Spark which enlightens all sides, a Brilliant Flame in the zenith of the heavens, **will teach thee that which thou dost not know of the facts of the universe and of the divine doctrine**. Verily, I say unto thee, every soul which ariseth today to guide others to the path of safety and infuse in them the Spirit of Life, the Holy Spirit will inspire that soul with evidences, proofs and facts and the lights will shine upon it from the Kingdom of God. Do not forget what I have conveyed unto thee from the breath of the Spirit. Verily, it is the shining morning and the rosy dawn which will impart unto thee the lights, **reveal the mysteries and make thee competent in science**, and through it the pictures of the Supreme World will be printed in thy heart and the facts of the secrets of the Kingdom of God will shine before thee.[7]

Scientists make painstaking progress by proceeding from 'step A to step B', by trial and error, collaborating with other scientists or reading the research of others. Along the way, it is undoubtedly true that flashes of intuition make possible the steady progression from A to B to C, etc., and it is also probable that some of those small intuitive leaps went unnoticed.

However, the spectacular leap of comprehension made by Melvin Calvin was the rule and not the exception in the lives of other famous scientists detailed in *Inner Knowing*. 'Abdu'l-Bahá has described in more detail the source of such incredible inspiration:

But the universal divine mind, which is beyond nature, is the bounty of the Preexistent Power. This universal mind is divine; it embraces existing realities, and it receives the light of the mysteries of God. It is a conscious power, not a power of investigation and of research. **The intellectual power of the world of nature is a power of investigation, and by its researches it discovers the realities of beings and the properties of existences**; but **the heavenly intellectual power, which is beyond nature, embraces things and is cognizant of things, knows them, understands them, is aware of mysteries, realities and divine significations, and is the discoverer of the concealed verities of the Kingdom**. This divine intellectual power is the special attribute of the Holy Manifestations and the Dawning-places of prophethood;

95

a ray of this light falls upon the mirrors of the hearts of the righteous, and a portion and share of this power comes to them from the Holy Manifestations.[8]

In the mirror of their minds the forms of transcendent realities are reflected, and the lamp of their inner vision derives its light from the sun of universal knowledge.[9]

The two quotations above explain that there are two extremely different sources of intelligence that are available to human beings. 'The intellectual power of nature' (of which man is a part) is a 'power of investigation'. The source is the human mind and this is the mind that receives training in our school systems. This mind proceeds logically from A to B to C, trying to 'discover the realities of beings' and 'the properties of existences'. Let's call this mental ability our **reasoning faculty**.

In the same quotation 'Abdu'l-Bahá states that we have access to 'the heavenly intellectual power which is beyond nature, embraces things and is cognizant of things'. Amazingly, the source of this 'power' is the 'universal divine mind', also referred to as the 'sun of universal knowledge' in the shorter quotation. At the end of the long quotation, 'Abdu'l-Bahá says, 'a ray of this light falls upon the mirrors of the hearts of the righteous, and a portion and share of this power comes to them from the Holy Manifestations'. Let's call this mental ability our **knowing faculty**.

The ramifications of the above statement should fill with awe and humility everyone with a hearing ear. Each individual on the planet has access to the mind of the Manifestation of God. Any of us who has experienced his own moment of life-changing inspiration now possesses personal proof that He is closer to us than our own life vein.

There was Melvin Calvin, waiting in his car for his wife when, much to his surprise, a complete picture that addressed all his questions appeared before him. 'Abdu'l-Bahá's promise that 'the pictures of the Supreme World will be printed in thy heart and the facts of the secrets of the Kingdom of God will shine before thee' proved to be true for Calvin, whose desire was to be 'competent in science'. What a shock it must have been for him, though. He was proceeding through A, B, C, D, E – and then, suddenly, made a leap all the way to Z.

However, it's important to also emphasize that Calvin didn't simply receive this answer as if by magic. He had also played the part required of him in the process. Had he not had the training and expertise in chemistry that he did and had he not asked the same questions, he would not have been able to access the information that was made available to him. We can only receive inspiration commensurate with the combination of our innate and acquired capacity.

Thus we need to strive for a balance between our reasoning and knowing faculties because an imbalance in these faculties creates a distortion in perception, and a distortion in perception leads to faulty decision-making.

A particular value of the two service questions is that the continued use of them over a long period of time tends to balance out all the known and unknown powers and faculties of the soul, including our knowing and reasoning faculties.

Here are some practical steps in using our inner faculties:

Step One: Use inner and outer faculties one at a time.

It is essential to understand that our outer and inner vision cannot be used simultaneously. The following three quotations support this reality:

> Bahá'u'lláh says there is a sign (from God) in every phenomenon: the sign of the intellect is contemplation and the sign of contemplation is silence, because it is impossible for a man to do two things at one time – he cannot both speak and meditate.[10]

> To illustrate this, think of man as endowed with two kinds of sight; when the power of insight is being used the outward power of vision does not see.[11]

> O Man of Two Visions! Close one eye and open the other. Close one to the world, and all that is therein and open the other to the hallowed beauty of the Beloved.[12]

When the reasoning faculties, which rely on the outer senses, are not able to provide answers, it is often helpful to shut those faculties down and look inward for the answers. Understanding that there is another way to get from D to E has a calming effect on our emotional state, a process we can assist through the use of prayer. We can also use whatever relaxation methods we may have found helpful, such as meditation, music or breathing that helps us to quiet ourselves.

Step Two: Ask questions.

In an extraordinary discourse recorded in *Paris Talks*, 'Abdu'l-Bahá referred to a Society of Friends in Persia, a group whose origins date back a thousand years.[13] He said that these 'Followers of the inner light' were 'entirely freed from blind dogmas and imitations'.[14] 'Abdu'l-Bahá stated that this process of accessing inspiration begins with the asking of a simple question and being open to whatever answer is received.

> It is an axiomatic fact that while you meditate you are speaking with your own spirit. In that state of mind you put certain **questions** to your spirit and the spirit answers: the light breaks forth and the reality is revealed.[15]

Here is how 'Abdu'l-Bahá explains the faculty of meditation:

> Through the faculty of meditation man attains to eternal life; through it he receives the breath of the Holy Spirit – the bestowal of the Spirit is given in reflection and meditation.
>
> The spirit of man is itself informed and strengthened during meditation; through it affairs of which man knew nothing are unfolded before his view. Through it he receives Divine inspiration, through it he receives heavenly food.
>
> Meditation is the key for opening the doors of mysteries. In that state man abstracts himself: in that state man withdraws himself from all outside objects; in that subjective mood he is immersed in the ocean of spiritual life and can unfold the secrets of things-in-themselves.[16]

Every time that we use the faculty of meditation, which, by 'Abdu'l-Bahá's definition, means that we ask a question directed inward to our own spirit instead of outward to another person, we are activating our intuitive knowing faculties.

Keeping in mind that the faculty of meditation is activated by asking an inner question and that this begins a process that is 'the key for opening the doors of mysteries', let's go back a few paragraphs and reread the quotation from 'Abdu'l-Bahá that begins 'But the universal divine mind'. This quotation explains that the 'divine intellectual power', which is the 'special attribute of the Holy Manifestations', illumines the 'mirrors of the hearts of the righteous' and it is this power that enables the individual to unravel the mysteries of the material and spiritual worlds. Therefore the key to accessing the universal divine mind, which is the source of all creativity and original ideas, is to ask a question of our own heart.

There is something amazing that happens when we use our faculty of meditation.

This faculty frees us from our animal nature, we are told. And when the animal nature is not in control of our life, we become free of 'blind dogmas and imitations', just like the 'Followers of the inner light' a thousand years ago in Persia.

And all of this happens just because we chose to ask an inner question. Not in the least coincidental is that the first step in using the two service questions is to ask ourselves a question:

1) At this moment in time, what is the act of service I am capable of giving that the other person is capable of receiving?

2) At this moment in time, what is the act of service I am capable of receiving that the other person is capable of giving?

'Abdu'l-Bahá says that we ask a question and we receive an answer. Sometimes, however, we are not consciously aware of having received an answer. There are a variety of reasons why this happens. One reason is that our reasoning faculty needs to be able to comprehend the inspiration. For example, 1961 Noble Laureate in Chemistry Melvin Calvin was able to receive his vision of discovery because of his education and experience.

Lest we think we have nothing in common with this great scientist, it is important to know that we have everything in common with his experience. For the average person, trying to maintain or repair a damaged relationship is just as daunting and requires a developed intuitive faculty. There are countless situations in the complexity of life that require more than the mental ability to add two and two.

Step Three: Listen.

Another reason we are sometimes unable to access inspiration is because of what might be called 'inner noise'. If we telephone a wise friend for advice and then rant and rave when that person tries to offer help, we won't be able to hear the answer. Or, if we pose a question to our self and then our ego insists on only one answer, this also creates inner noise that will then mask the real answer. Just as outer noise makes it impossible to hear, inner noise, in the form of negative emotions, impressions or beliefs, makes it impossible to hear inspiration. Inner noise will be explored further in the next chapter on the human mind.

Step Four: Identify the best time to receive inspiration.

This leads to another important part of the process. Is there a time of the day when we are less likely to experience inner noise and therefore more likely to receive inspiration? For some, what works best is early morning, as suggested in the following prayer of Bahá'u'lláh. However, it is important to bear in mind that each of us needs to figure out this question of timing for ourselves and discover what works best within our own lives.

> I give praise to Thee, O my God, that Thou hast awakened me out of my sleep, and brought me forth after my disappearance, and raised me up from my slumber . . .
> I beseech Thee, by the potency of Thy will and the compelling power of Thy purpose, to make of what Thou didst reveal unto me in my sleep the surest foundation for the mansions of Thy love that are within the hearts of Thy loved ones, and the best instrument for the revelation of the tokens of Thy grace and Thy loving-kindness.[17]

Step Five: Be 'home' when the inspiration arrives.

By 'home' is not meant a physical dwelling but rather the spiritual equivalent, which is the place of our relationship with God and of our identity and purpose – our heart. Imagine how badly we would feel if we invited a distinguished guest to our home and when she knocked on the door there was no one home.

> O Son of Being! Thy Paradise is My love; **thy heavenly home, reunion with Me.** Enter therein and tarry not. This is that which hath been destined for thee in Our kingdom above and Our exalted Dominion.[18]

'Home' here is defined as 'reunion with Me'. The only relationship with God sanctioned in the Bahá'í writings for those mortals living in the condition of servitude is that of a servant of God. That is our identity/purpose and it is our 'spiritual address'. That 'home', our heart, is where the ray of light from the universal divine mind will be sent.

Nader Saiedi in his book *Gate of the Heart: Understanding the Writings of the Báb* says, 'When the station of servitude is realized, then the divine light will shine upon the pure mirror of the heart.'[19]

It is important to be conscious of our true identity as a servant of God when asking and receiving inspiration – indeed to be conscious of who we really are every moment of our life.

Step Six: Empower inspiration with acts of service.

Our inner faculties need the sustenance of a spiritual power source, just as our outer faculties require the sustaining nourishment of physical food. The steps we take in service are a part of what helps to empower our inner faculties, as this passage reminds us:

> Verily, I say unto thee, every soul which ariseth today to guide others to the path of safety and infuse in them the Spirit of Life, the Holy Spirit will inspire that soul with evidences, proofs and facts and the lights will shine upon it from the Kingdom of God.[20]

Rúḥíyyih Khánum shared another story at the Bahá'í World Congress in 1992 about a visit that she and her mother, May Maxwell, received from fellow Bahá'í Martha Root at their home in Montreal in 1926. Martha lived 'to guide others to the path of safety and infuse them with the Spirit of Life' and she had a great effect and influence on hearts everywhere she went in the world.

May Maxwell and Martha Root decided to call on the manager of the new radio station in Montreal, believing that the new medium of radio could help spread the message of Bahá'u'lláh more effectively.

As they were leaving the house, Martha noticed a vase of tulips near the door and, without explanation, took one tulip out of the vase.

When the women were introduced to the manager of the radio station, he enquired as to the purpose of their visit.

Martha Root stepped forward and said, 'I came to give you this tulip.'

The manager began to cry, while gently cradling the tulip in his hands.

'I am a native of Holland and this flower reminds me of my homeland,' he told them.

The manager was instantly ready to grant whatever requests the women had.

This story illustrates the principle that what in the beginning is seen as difficult and almost unnatural can eventually become natural and effortless. Think of watching a great concert pianist and observing how her fingers move with grace and impossible speed. The performance looked nothing like that the first few times she sat down at a piano.

Step Seven: Cleanse your heart.

Let's take another look at the quotation about the universal divine mind:

> . . . a ray of this light falls upon the mirrors of the **hearts** of the righteous, and a portion and a share of this power comes to them through the Holy Manifestations.[21]

The following passages, one a ḥadíth quoted by Bahá'u'lláh and the other from a talk of 'Abdu'l-Bahá given in London, also describe that it is the heart that is the recipient of this kind of inner knowing:

> Knowledge is a light which God casteth into the heart of whomsoever He willeth.[22]

> But if you turn the mirror of your spirits heavenwards, the heavenly constellations and the rays of the Sun of Reality will be reflected in your hearts, and the virtues of the Kingdom will be obtained.[23]

The following quotation from the Seven Valleys comes from the Valley of Search, which Bahá'u'lláh designates as the first valley in our spiritual journey. This passage appears right at the beginning of the Valley of Search and reads as though the actions set out are required for continuing on through the Seven Valleys. Bahá'u'lláh specifically counsels that we must 'cleanse' ourselves from imitation or we cannot make this journey.

> It is incumbent on these servants that they **cleanse the heart – which is the wellspring of divine treasures** – from every marking, and that they turn away from imitation, which is following the traces of their forefathers and sires . . .[24]

Bahá'u'lláh has now also supplied us with a definition of the human heart: the 'wellspring of divine treasures'.

The second quotation is from what is commonly called the Tablet of the True Seeker, and once again, Bahá'u'lláh appears to be defining the heart in this way. He even uses the word 'cleanse' again.

> But, O my brother, when a true seeker determineth to take the step of search in the path leading to the knowledge of the Ancient of Days, he must, before all else, cleanse and purify his heart, which is the **seat of the revelation of the inner mysteries of God** . . .[25]

In each of these passages Bahá'u'lláh seems to be counseling that the first step required on the spiritual path is to cleanse ourselves from imitation. That is why this book's earliest chapters deal with the critical necessity of freeing ourselves from imitation, since a true spiritual journey requires unfettered free will, clear vision and a truly attentive ear. The two service questions, to be effective, rely on the use of our free will. We cannot be a captive to blind imitation and hope to grow spiritually.

What else can prevent the inspiration of the universal divine mind from reaching our heart, the 'wellspring of divine treasures'?

> The favours of God are all-surrounding, but should the conscious eye of the soul of man remain veiled and darkened, he will be led to deny these universal signs and remain deprived of these manifestations of

divine bounty. Therefore, we must endeavour with heart and soul in order that the veil covering the eye of inner vision may be removed, that we may behold the manifestations of the signs of God, discern His mysterious graces and realize that material blessings as compared with spiritual bounties are as nothing.[26]

This quotation says that if our inner vision is veiled, we cannot perceive 'the signs of God'. We know from a previous quotation that the spirit of faith is needed to understand spiritual realities. We also understand that if we obey the Manifestation of God, and that obedience is translated into acts of service that are in harmony with the Covenant of God, we will be imbued with the spirit of faith, which enables us to understand spiritual realities.

However, if we do not know we are servants of God and are not engaged in acts of service, then we drift off the path of reality and find ourselves lost in a world of illusion. Illusory acts create veils that prevent us from receiving and understanding revelation. Such acts cause us to become attached to everything but God. Each attachment acts like a particle of dust on the mirror of our heart.

Wert thou to cleanse the mirror of thy heart from the dust of malice, thou wouldst apprehend the meaning of the symbolic terms revealed by the all-embracing Word of God made manifest in every Dispensation, and wouldst discover the mysteries of divine knowledge.[27]

When we accumulate enough particles of dust on the mirror of our heart, we have created a veil. Now, as we look at what we have been told about the potential of the human heart, we see that as the 'wellspring of divine treasures' it is the destined home of the two sources of knowledge available to every human being. These are the reasoning faculty, whose source is the human mind, and the knowing faculty, whose source is the 'universal divine mind' of the Manifestations of God. Ideally, the heart is the place where a consultation between all the inner and outer powers and faculties occurs.

We have also seen that the heart, when animated by the spirit of faith, obeys its divine purpose by conceiving and carrying out acts of service illumined by and arising out of the infinite attributes of God and guided by the eternal Covenant of God.

Step Eight: Confirm that inspiration is in harmony with the Covenant.

Once we have posed our inner question and received our answer, it's helpful to also remember that we are fallible human beings and can therefore never be sure that the inspiration is valid. By valid we mean that the inspiration must be in harmony with the Covenant of God.

For example, if our inner question was, 'How do I patch up a quarrel with my friend?' and the answer received was, 'Punch him in the nose', we can assume that our inspiration was not genuine. Our ultimate check-and-balance is to take the inspiration and use it to give or receive an act of service that is in harmony with the Covenant.

Neither the inner or outer faculties by themselves are capable of the 'increasingly complex acts of service' called for by the Universal House of Justice. Only the heart is capable of forming and sustaining the deeper spiritual relationships that we all crave to have with our fellow servants of God. Only the heart is capable of knowing 'how they should act towards one another'.

Step Nine: Trust in God and trust in the process.

While, at first, these steps may seem a cumbersome process, with use they can actually become lightning-fast. An answer to the inner question of what would be an appropriate act of service can come in a matter of seconds. After all, the spiritual world is not bound by time.

The authors have wondered why there is so much information in the Bahá'í writings about inner vision and how we receive inspiration. We have come to the conclusion that there is some deep connection between these abilities and the Covenant of God as Bahá'u'lláh has revealed it in this day. This wonderful power of the faculty of inner vision can now be safely used within the framework of this new, unbreakable Covenant, thus mitigating possible misuses of our spiritual senses. The authors wish to particularly acknowledge the enormous contributions of author Henry Weil, who in clear and simple language explains the faculty of inner vision in his two books, *Closer Than Your Life-vein* and *Drops from the Ocean*.

Diane notes that inner vision experiences are among her favourites in life. They occur in those rare moments when we feel as though we are like a leaf carried on a stream, or perhaps we feel irresistibly drawn towards something, or even seem to be funnelled in a direction from which there seems no escape. While we still have the obligation to make sure that our inspiration is in harmony with the Covenant, it is wonderful to feel that the Unseen Realm is at hand.

One of Phyllis's favourite inner vision experiences came in connection with an article she wrote about Dolores Kendrick, the gifted writer who has served for many years as Washington DC's poet laureate. The experience reinforced for her the reality that when our material and spiritual purposes are in sync, a kind of spiritual reciprocity seems to flow from that.

After several interviews with Dolores, Phyllis wrote an article that was scheduled to run in a magazine with a fairly large national circulation. By this time Dolores had also become a kind and mentoring friend in Phyllis's life.

Then Phyllis received word that the magazine had undergone a change in leadership and was going to scrap the article. It was deeply disappointing news and she couldn't find the will to call and tell Dolores that day. She went to bed that night with prayers and the intention to 'turn it over'.

The next morning she awoke with the thought of another similar publication, one actually better established, with an even larger circulation. Something seemed to be saying very directly: 'Contact them now.'

The email query she sent that day brought a response within the hour. The editor had taken a look at the manuscript and rapidly accepted it to fill a space that had suddenly opened up in his magazine's very next issue.

Phyllis called Dolores with this far happier news, astonished by this turnaround hand-delivered by the universe. But she didn't know half of it.

About a week after that article was published, the dean of an East Coast university saw it and called to ask how he might contact Dolores to invite her to be the university's commencement speaker that year. In addition, because hers was such a long and distinguished career, the university also wanted to award Dolores an honorary master's degree.

For Phyllis, this particular experience was all the more profound because the gifts of inner vision presented themselves at a time when things could have looked the most discouraging.

Only the spiritual nature with its comprehension of material and spiritual reality is capable of blending the information from our reasoning and knowing faculties and then using that knowledge to create unique acts of service.

Let's recap what we have learned in this chapter by adding a facet to our Options Chart.

The Options Chart

Facet to be considered in determining an act of service	Optional	Not Optional	Chapter
Must be guided by both the power of investigation and inner vision (requires listening, even to silence)		X	8

The whole, completed Options Chart can be found in appendix 1.

9

SERVANT TO TRUTH

The Mind Animated by the Spirit of Faith

> God has not intended man to blindly imitate . . . He has endowed him with mind, or the faculty of reasoning . . . to investigate and discover truth, and that which he finds real and true he must accept. He must not be an imitator or blind follower . . .[1]

> But the human spirit, unless assisted by the spirit of faith, does not become acquainted with the **divine secrets** and the **heavenly realities** . . . the mind is the power of the human spirit.[2]

Again, in its letter of 19 November 1974, the Universal House explained that in order for souls to fulfil their created purpose:

1) They need to know who they are.

2) They need to know to what purpose they exist.

3) **They need to know how they should act towards one another.**

4) They need to be helped to gradually apply these answers to everyday behaviour.

How can our mind, the faculty of reasoning designed to help us investigate and discover truth, be assisted to abandon time-worn blind imitations and investigate reality? The spirit of faith is the means because it allows the mind to attain to the highest level of perception required for the investigation of spiritual as well as material aspects of reality. None of the four questions listed above could be fully answered by an individual animated solely by the human spirit.

The quality of the decisions we make depends on the successful investigation of our own reality, the reality of our fellow servants and the reality of our relationship with God, all of which are 'divine secrets' and 'heavenly realities'.

It follows then that the wisdom needed to give and receive 'progressively more complex and demanding acts of service' requires individuals to be animated by the spirit of faith.

'Abdu'l-Bahá has explained that all meaning is found within the Covenant of God, the most powerful force in the universe. In fact, He says, the universe does not contain this Covenant, nor does the Covenant serve the universe. The exact opposite is true.

> Today, the Lord of Hosts is the defender of the Covenant, the forces of the Kingdom protect it, heavenly souls tender their services, and heavenly angels promulgate and spread it broadcast. **If it is considered with insight, it will be seen that all the forces of the universe, in the last analysis serve the Covenant.**[3]

This new Covenant brought by Bahá'u'lláh contains elements never before seen in previous religious dispensations, including the appearance of 'Abdu'l-Bahá as the Exemplar of the teachings brought by the Manifestation of God, the role of the Guardianship of the Faith, the administrative order, and voluminous sacred texts on every subject.

When we attempt to figure out how we 'should act towards one another' and to formulate an act of service, our mind, aided by the spirit of faith, needs to decide what element of the Covenant is particularly relevant. Perhaps it is the spiritual guidance in a phrase from a prayer or sacred writings and other inspiration, or the example of 'Abdu'l-Bahá.

Yet even as it is animated by the spirit of faith, the mind also needs to rely on the heart, guided by the spiritual nature, as it formulates unique acts of service. The reader may want to refer back to the previous chapter to read how the writings define 'heart'. The role that the heart plays will be explored in more depth in the next and last chapter on the spiritual nature.

One means of conveying the concept that all meaning is found within the Covenant is through diagrams composed of concentric circles. The outermost circle always represents the Covenant. This is symbolic of the fact that everything is contained within the Covenant and not the other way around, that 'all the forces of the universe serve the Covenant'.

To make this reality more concrete, imagine a room full of people all more than seven feet tall when a person six feet tall joins the group. In the context of this particular group, this person could be considered short. However, if the same person joined a group of individuals who were five feet tall, the six-footer would be considered tall.

The key word in this situation is 'context'. Context provides meaning but in a world in which the context is ever-changing, meaning becomes elusive. If we sum up in one word what the people of the world 'desperately need to know', that word is 'meaning'. Meaning doesn't disappear or change, like the shifting sands beneath our feet, and the source of this consistent, unchanging meaning is the Covenant of God.

In the previous chapter we talked about the impediment to the efficient use of our knowledge-gathering faculties that we call inner noise. We live in a new era of continual guidance from the sacred writings and up-to-the-minute infallible guidance from the Universal House of Justice. The more we structure our lives around this guidance, the more clarity of mind we'll experience and the less distracting that inner noise will be.

The remainder of this chapter will provide a variety of examples that demonstrate this concept. Each highlights a common problem that often occurs between two people in a relationship and seeks to illustrate the role of the mind – animated by the spirit of faith – in finding a solution.

But first, let's revisit the two service questions that help us formulate the action steps needed to investigate reality and then carry out acts of service:

1) At this moment in time, what is the act of service I am capable of giving that the other person is capable of receiving?

2) At this moment in time, what is the act of service I am capable of receiving that the other person is capable of giving?

Describing an incident in his book *Three Minute Therapy*, therapist Dr Michael Edelstein recalls a young couple locked in a battle of egos that was ruining their relationship. The wife demanded that her husband be seated at the dinner table every night at 6:00 p.m. and the husband reacted to her demands by coming home later and later. Their relationship was unravelling.

Dr Edelstein's solution was to have each of them write, 'I am not the lord of the universe' over and over again on a pad of paper. He also asked them to change their demanding words and tones from 'you must' to 'I prefer'.

The soul knows that it is a servant of God and that God is not a husband or wife. Being confronted by someone who seems to be acting like an all-powerful deity provokes a negative reaction that can take many forms because the soul's true identity and relationship with God have been challenged. But with the simple substitution of the words 'I prefer', this situation was defused, the battle of wills subsided as interaction between two souls became more respectful and their relationship gradually improved.

Down deep, we naturally recoil when we perceive that mere mortals act towards us as though they are the lord of the universe and we are one of their subjects. As souls, our higher nature also recoils when our own human will takes this approach towards others and we seek advantage over them in some way.

If we take this suggestion of Dr Edelstein's to heart and apply it in all our relationships, such simple changes as saying, 'I prefer' or 'Perhaps it's worth considering . . .' can set a whole new tone in our interactions. After all, we are responsible for our own spiritual development and path of service and not anyone else's. When we say 'prefer', we are giving the other person full recognition as another unique soul and servant of God.

The couple in this story were helped to understand who they were NOT, which is a far cry from knowing who they ARE. For a relationship to grow past the survival stage and thrive, it must be based on a positive and not a negative foundation.

The underlying spiritual principle involved is that we are servants of God and servants of God do not seek to control another person's life. In fact, we simply cannot do so.

Generally speaking, the role of an enlightened mind is to focus the energy of the individual on goals consistent with being a servant of God living within the Covenant of God. Trying to live a life consistent with the Covenant establishes healthy parameters for our relationship with God, the Manifestation of God and our fellow servants of God. The Covenant is a standard that establishes what is acceptable in our various relationships and what is not acceptable. More importantly, the Covenant provides the overall meaning to our life that we all desperately seek. 'All the forces of the universe serve the Covenant' because the Covenant provides the meaning for every atom of existence.

We suggest that every interaction between the individual and any of what we are referring to as the elements of the Covenant contributes to the building of healthy parameters for all our relationships by providing lasting meaning to those relationships.

In the above illustration the Covenant of Bahá'u'lláh, which offers the overall context that can provide meaning, is represented as the outermost circle. The inner circle is labelled 'Servant of God'. According to the guidance from 'Abdu'l-Bahá, there is no real meaning outside the context of the Covenant:

> Today, the Lord of Hosts is the defender of the Covenant, the forces of the Kingdom protect it, heavenly souls tender their services, and heavenly angels promulgate and spread it broadcast. **If it is considered with insight, it will be seen that all the forces of the universe, in the last analysis serve the Covenant.**[4]

This applies whether the inner circle is Servant of God, love, justice or a principle like the equality of men and women.

These words and phrases are only morally neutral 'syllables and sounds'. We may be puzzled at this suggestion and say, 'But isn't love an attribute of God?'

Yet what if someone 'loves' to drink alcohol and drive, or 'loves' to deface or destroy property? Could we ever call such love an attribute of God? Love or justice or mercy are merely human qualities and do not rise to the level of an attribute of God unless they are embedded in an act of service that is consistent with the Covenant.

This means that acts of service, to be effective, need to be generated by a servant of God as defined by the Covenant. It is the responsibility of the mind to remind the individual that no matter the decision to be made or the problem to be solved, the best chance to come up with a successful act of service to improve the situation is for a servant of God to ask the inner service questions.

The following example illustrates how interacting with an element of the Covenant moulds and transforms all of our inner and outer faculties. This process begins with the mind recognizing what those elements of the Covenant are. In this example, the element of the Covenant that the mind comes into contact with is divine law.

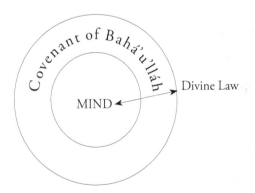

There will be times when we will encounter a law revealed by the Manifestation of God that we do not understand or that we are, for the moment, unwilling to accept. Ron recalls one such experience.

Among the laws of the Bahá'í Faith, Bahá'u'lláh has forbidden the drinking of alcohol. When Ron declared his belief in Bahá'u'lláh, he hadn't read a single Bahá'í book. His decision was motivated by the spirit he felt from Bahá'í friends gathered at Green Acre Bahá'í School in Maine, and, he believed, the lingering presence of the visit that 'Abdu'l-Bahá had made there in 1912. He was in high school at the time and before he went to Green Acre with his family, he was drinking alcohol. It didn't matter what he drank, he loved it all.

Ron declared his faith in a matter of days and worked that summer at Green Acre, which changed his life forever. He returned to school that fall for his senior year and informed his former drinking buddies that he had given up alcohol. He told them that it was a law of his new religion that he was determined to follow but he couldn't explain the wisdom of the law when they asked what was so wrong with a few beers on the weekend. He did, however, accept the reality that the Manifestation of God had a vastly superior intelligence. Ron's responsibility was to obey and keep learning every day.

A few years later, he became friends with a co-worker whose husband's alcoholism was destroying the family. She knew Ron was a Bahá'í and that he believed it was potentially destructive to use alcohol, even in moderation. She asked him the same questions that his friends in high school had asked years earlier. What was wrong with a few drinks every now and then? Why should she have to give up her social drinking simply because her husband was an alcoholic?

This time Ron explained that the laws of this age are based on the principle of the oneness of humankind. He told her that science has informed us that in every society where alcohol has been introduced, 20 to 30 per cent of the population will experience a negative impact from it, either directly or indirectly. He then asked his friend what would happen if she and her husband had eight children. Would they introduce alcohol into their family of ten knowing that there would be a high probability that two or three of her children's lives, or one or both of the parents' lives, would be ruined? Was the enjoyment that seven members of their family would derive from moderate social drinking worth potential – and significant – damage to the lives of the other three family members?

Ron's friend actually agreed with his reasoning and said that if she could start all over again, she would do everything she could to have an alcohol-free home. Ron never knew whether what he shared helped change the dynamics of this particular family but he did know that he was able to offer a reasonable answer to the question. He later realized that the quality of his life – even his life itself – had been saved because he was able to obey a law he did not understand.

This is not an argument for blind obedience, however. It is important that we try to understand the wisdom behind divine laws. Yet the act of obedience, in and of itself, is a powerful pathway to understanding the wisdom of the law. That's because the act of obedience attracts the spirit of faith, which enables the mind to understand more of spiritual reality. Also, when we have a positive experience with obeying one law that we find difficult to understand, we can build on that experience and gain the confidence or strength to obey other laws that we find difficult.

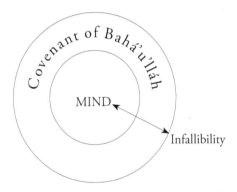

This next example is related to the previous one. In the diagram above, an arrow leads from the mind to another element of the Covenant, the concept of infallibility. We know the source of the laws we are given is infallible.

Imagine that we are sitting with a friend reading the following Hidden Word of Bahá'u'lláh together:

O My Friends! Have ye forgotten that true and radiant morn, when in those hallowed and blessed surroundings ye were gathered in My presence beneath the shade of the tree of life, which is planted in the all-glorious paradise? Awe-struck ye listened as I gave utterance to these three most holy words: O friends! Prefer not your will to Mine, never desire that which I have not desired for you, and approach Me not with lifeless hearts, defiled with worldly desires and cravings. Would ye but sanctify your souls, ye would at this present hour recall that place and those surroundings, and the truth of My utterance should be made evident unto all of you.[5]

Then imagine that, as we begin discussing the possible meaning of this Hidden Word, 'Abdu'l-Bahá walks into the room and sits down. The key question here is, would we continue to share our opinions or would we defer to 'Abdu'l-Bahá and listen with respect to what He had to say first? Since in His Covenant Bahá'u'lláh named 'Abdu'l-Bahá the authorized interpreter of His teachings, the Word of God, it follows that He would offer an infallible explanation and that it would be very beneficial to receive it.

The simple act of waiting to activate our mind until after we consult the guidance in the sacred writings fosters a healthy discipline. This is the same procedure that the Universal House of Justice follows whenever it formulates a decision on any matter. It conducts thorough research to find out what the Central Figures of the Bahá'í Faith and Shoghi Effendi, the Guardian, have to say that is pertinent to the matter under consideration before it contemplates any decision.

> Today, the Universal House of Justice, before taking decisions on various matters whether in the field of legislation or administration, consults the writings of Shoghi Effendi and is guided by the vast body of his letters, in which he has elucidated almost every conceivable subject.[6]

> . . . a careful study of the Writings and interpretations on any subject on which the House of Justice proposes to legislate always precedes its act of legislation.[7]

So what did 'Abdu'l-Bahá tell us? The explanation He provided that helps to reveal the meaning in this particular Hidden Word is cited in volume one of Taherzadeh's *The Revelation of Bahá'u'lláh*.[8] 'Abdu'l-Bahá explained that the 'true and radiant morn' refers to the Revelation of the Báb and the 'hallowed and blessed surroundings' refers to the heart of the individual. The overall theme of the Hidden Word, according to 'Abdu'l-Bahá, is the establishment of the Covenant of Bahá'u'lláh (the 'tree of life' is a reference to Bahá'u'lláh as the Manifestation of God).

How often do we assume or construe meaning without making the time to investigate what sacred guidance offers us? How often, then, do we suffer needlessly or, at the very least, waste time and effort when we could be more effective?

When the fallible mind experiences the limitless possibilities of infallible First Mind, it awakens true humility in the heart. This can influence for the better every act of service for the rest of our life.

Thus our next example illustrates the interaction between the mind and another element of the Covenant: consultation.

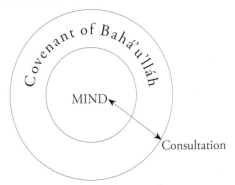

Consultation

In the diagram above an arrow links the role of the mind to that vital element of the Covenant, consultation. This is the divinely bestowed tool that offers us the opportunity to discipline our minds so that they can act in genuine and willing balance with our hearts in acts of real service.

In addition, consultation also enables and empowers us to work collectively with others' minds and hearts towards the purpose of human unity. Bahá'u'lláh has said of it:

> Consultation bestoweth greater awareness and transmuteth conjecture into certitude. It is a shining light which, in a dark world, leadeth the way and guideth. For everything there is and will continue to be a station of perfection and maturity. The maturity of the gift of understanding is made manifest through consultation.[9]

When it is used to solve problems, the kind of consultation that Bahá'u'lláh has outlined shares the same goals as consultation that is used in the world of human affairs. But the higher goal of this element of the Covenant is to achieve both a solution AND unity. In fact, we are told that if a decision is arrived at in unity and is wrong, it will be put right.

The first step in the process of consultation is to ascertain the truth of a situation and then identify what spiritual principles apply. 'Abdu'l-Bahá says:

> They must in every situation search out the truth and not insist upon their own opinion . . .[10]

We believe that 'Abdu'l-Bahá is telling us that we need to wait to form our personal opinion until after the establishment of the facts or the 'truth'. He does not say don't have an opinion, only that we need to establish things in their correct order. In a world devoid of divine guidance, this sense of sequence is being lost, which is harmful to the proper functioning of the mind. Identifying the relevant spiritual principle(s) leads inevitably to an interaction with the elements of the Covenant, as this is the source of those principles. It doesn't matter whether the consultation is between a small group of friends or practised by a local or national institution, the procedure is the same.

Let's look at the gifts that the Bahá'í writings tell us consultation bestows upon the world:[11]

1) Consultation is the lamp of guidance.
2) Consultation is the bestower of understanding.
3) Consultation is one of the most fundamental elements of the divine edifice.
4) Consultation results in light.
5) Consultation attracts the grace of the Holy Spirit.
6) Consultation attracts the hosts of divine confirmation.
7) Consultation has an effect upon the whole world.
8) Consultation will lead a world to eternal happiness.
9) Consultation allows the Hosts of the Supreme Concourse to render us victorious.
10) Consultation transforms the clash of thoughts into brilliant illumination.
11) Consultation sheds light on the facts involved.

12) Consultation is one of the most potent instruments conducive to the tranquillity and felicity of the people.
13) Consultation gives insight.
14) Consultation enables us to delve into questions that are unknown.
15) Consultation allows the light of truth to shine from our faces.
16) Consultation helps us to penetrate to the depths of each problem.
17) Consultation makes it possible to find the right solution.

During a discussion about what refreshments should be served at a public meeting, we sometimes lose sight of the fact that the benefits of engaging in the process of consultation are often more important than what is being decided. This is especially true when we read that 'consultation will lead a world to eternal happiness'.

It is worth reviewing this admittedly incomplete list of the benefits of consultation and then reflecting on how consultation helps us use the two service questions to investigate reality and to address those four key questions posed by the Universal House of Justice about our identity, purpose and behaviour – the essentials of our own reality, as a soul.

For example: How does 'insight' help formulate acts of service? Or how does being able to 'penetrate to the depths of each problem' contribute to figuring out how we 'should act towards one another'?

In *Developing Genius*, one of two books he has written about the role of consultation, author John Kolstoe describes synergy, a process in which the sum is greater than its parts. Through consultation, the possibility exists of a superior solution emerging from the group whose powers are greater than any that individuals are capable of achieving on their own.

In exploring the power of consultation even on the level of the most practical material decisions, an exercise used in military training demonstrates the clear advantage of group thinking. Participants broke into groups of six to eight and were given a hypothetical example from training procedures followed by US Navy pilots who are forced to abandon an aircraft owing to an emergency. The situation requires them to make a quick decision about what items to transfer from the plane to a life raft. Since the raft is small, pilots can choose only ten essential items to bring along.

In the first part of the exercise each individual in the small groups chooses ten items. Students then reconvene in their groups and consult together to create a group list of ten items. About six small groups did this exercise and in each case the group's list of items came closer to the Navy's official priority list than did the lists compiled by individuals. This exercise was created by the Navy to convince personnel that the wisdom that resulted from group consultation was greater than the wisdom of any one individual. Of course, there are always exceptions but the Navy had found this principle to be generally true.

There are times in all our lives when the problem at hand is simply overwhelming and it can be a lonely struggle to come up with a solution. The principle of consultation offers a tool that is both effective and empowering. When we gather some trusted friends together to consult about a problem in our life or a decision about our future, the very fact of sharing with close friends lessens the stress and makes it easier to benefit from the synergy created.

The writings of the Bahá'í Faith continually remind us that outer circumstances reflect inner ones. While we may be familiar with outward consultation, what are the workings of inner consultation?

Through outward consultation the mind is trained to detach from and release its ideas to the group and thereby surrender attachment to and ownership of the ideas. But in order for this process to work, the heart must also undergo training on an even deeper level, and this training of the heart must precede the training of the mind.

A requisite is 'a required or necessary thing; a thing needed for a purpose'.

> The prime **requisites** for them that take counsel together are purity of motive, radiance of spirit, detachment from all else save God, attraction to His Divine Fragrances, humility and lowliness amongst His loved ones, patience and long-suffering in difficulties and servitude to His exalted Threshold. Should they be graciously aided to acquire these attributes, victory from the unseen Kingdom of Bahá shall be vouchsafed to them.[12]

The requisites enumerated here are:

1) Purity of motive
2) Radiance of spirit

3) Detachment from all else save God
4) Attraction to His Divine Fragrances
5) Humility and lowliness amongst His loved ones
6) Patience and long-suffering in difficulties
7) Servitude to His exalted Threshold

Before we engage in outward consultation together, our reasoning and knowing faculties must engage in inner consultation and be motivated by 'purity of motive'. They must also be filled with the 'radiance of spirit', be detached from all save God, be attracted to His divine fragrances, exhibit 'humility and lowliness among His loved ones', demonstrate 'patience and long-suffering in difficulties'. And finally, they must manifest 'servitude to His exalted Threshold'.

Our faculties are then prepared to properly use the attributes of God that reside in our hearts, 'the wellspring of divine treasures', in acts of service consistent with the Covenant of God. All of this essential activity takes place within the 'hallowed and blessed surroundings' of the heart.

In both inner and outer consultation it is essential that the process of synergy, in which the whole is greater than the sum of its parts, be maintained.

Obviously, while consulting with others is beneficial, it would be impossible to do this for every act of service we give or receive. We can and should engage in inner consultation. We have our mind and reason to assess a situation. We have spiritual guidance to keep us on the right path. We have the insight brought about through prayer and meditation in which we consult with our own spirit. Finding ourselves alone is no impediment to giving or receiving effective and potent acts of service.

Inner Consultation and Conceptual Thinking

As we consider the role of inner consultation in the investigation of reality, it is helpful to reflect once more on conceptual thinking. This has been defined previously as the ability to identify patterns or connections between information and/or situations that do not appear to be related.

Within this process of investigation, it's important to recognize the difference between facts and concepts. Facts are simple indicators of individual pieces of information, while more complex concepts offer a wider, overall view that can lead the way to deeper understanding and wisdom.

Often we assume that we've arrived at a concept when, in actuality, we haven't ascertained all the facts. Inner consultation, the engaging of all our powers and faculties – known and unknown – will, at the very least, slow the entire process down and prevent a rush to a premature and too often erroneous conclusion.

Here is an example from the Bahá'í writings:

> But with the human soul, there is no decline. Its only movement is towards perfection; growth and progress alone constitute the motion of the soul.[13]

It would be understandable after reading the above quotation to believe that we had a complete concept but we would be mistaken. Please read the next quotation:

> In this material world time has cycles; places change through alternating seasons, and for souls there are progress, retrogression and education.[14]

The first quotation says that souls only experience endless progression. The second quotation seems to contradict the first by stating 'retrogression' is possible. Although this quotation refers to souls in this world, we also know that 'The Celestial Universe is so formed that the under world reflects the upper world. That is to say whatever exists in heaven is reflected in this phenomenal world.'[15] '. . . the outward is the expression of the inward; the earth is the mirror of the Kingdom; the material world corresponds to the spiritual world.'[16]

Albert Einstein is reported to have said that to transition from fact-based thinking to concept-based thinking it is necessary to pass through a stage where the facts seem to be contradictory. He went on to say that only after all seeming contradictions are reconciled does one arrive at a genuine concept.

The seeming contradiction in the quotations above is reconciled by the following quotation:

> Now, as the spirit continues to exist after death, it necessarily progresses

or declines; and in the other world to cease to progress is the same as to decline . . .[17]

The dawn finally breaks as the two passages are reconciled: not growing is the same as declining, If we had only read the first quotation, we would have made the premature and mistaken leap from fact to concept.

Let's take this a step further. If we meditate on the three quotations, the dawn will not only break, the noon day sun will begin to shine brightly. 'Abdu'l-Bahá is saying that in the next world, a purely spiritual world, if we fail to make progress, we will decline. Doesn't this imply that our free will still has a role to play in our growth in the next world?

When we don't independently investigate reality for ourselves, we fall into the trap of blind imitation. In the last example of the three quotations we actually had the advantage of legitimate facts. In the following example we see the damage done by blind imitation when we begin with an incorrect premise – specifically the erroneous notion that we do not grow by our own efforts in the next world.

We will begin with how Bahá'í author and scholar Dr John Hatcher addresses this in his book *The Purpose of Physical Reality*.

He describes how it is possible to find references in works about the Bahá'í Faith that imply that the end of the physical life is the end of our opportunity to strive for enlightenment and growth. From such inferences, he notes, we might come to believe

. . . that in the afterlife there is no will, no independence of thought, no way to express the desire to progress. Such an inference would seem to be corroborated by 'Abdu'l-Bahá's statement that it is 'possible' that the condition of a sinner may become changed in the next world, but only through God's mercy:

It is even possible that the condition of those who have died in sin and unbelief may become changed – that is to say, they may become the object of pardon through the bounty of God, not through His justice – for bounty is giving without desert, and justice is giving what is deserved.[18]

Dr Hatcher overturns this common misunderstanding by employing a quotation by 'Abdu'l-Bahá:

As we have power to pray for these souls here, so likewise we shall possess the same power in the other world, which is the Kingdom of God. Are not all the people in that world the creatures of God? Therefore, in that world also they can make progress. As here they can receive light by their supplications, there also they can plead for forgiveness and receive light through entreaties and supplications.[19]

Dr Hatcher makes his point:

We can hardly fail to recognize that to supplicate, to plead, to make entreaties are actions that require free will on the part of those who have died in sin.[20]

Now let's trace the origin of this widespread misconception which, the authors assert, can be traced to a misunderstanding of a chapter of *Some Answered Questions*:

Question: After the body is put aside and the spirit has obtained freedom, in what way will the **rational soul** exist? Let us suppose that the **souls** who are assisted by the bounty of the Holy Spirit attain to true existence and eternal life. But what becomes of the rational souls – that is to say, the veiled spirits.[21]

Before we get to 'Abdu'l-Bahá's answer, notice that the questioner, Laura Clifford Barney, isn't worried about the fate of 'souls' in the next world. Remember she said, 'Let us suppose that the souls who are assisted by the bounty of the Holy Spirit attain to true existence and eternal life.' She is concerned for '**rational souls**' which she calls 'veiled spirits' and which 'here signify rational souls, souls not possessing the spirit of faith'. She is expressing concern not for the fate of 'souls', only rational souls.

Here is another clarifying quotation from 'Abdu'l-Bahá:

Now these 'spirits' are not reckoned as Spirit in the terminology of the Scriptures and the usage of the people of the Truth, inasmuch as the laws governing them are as the laws which govern all phenomenal being in respect to generation, corruption, production, change and reversion, as is clearly indicated in the Gospel where it says: 'Let the dead bury their dead' . . . inasmuch as he who would bury these dead was alive with the vegetative, animal and **rational human soul**, yet did Christ – to whom be glory! – declare such dead and devoid of life, in that this person was devoid of the **spirit of faith**, which is of the Kingdom of God. [22]

A **rational soul** that enters the next world finds itself in a purely spiritual world that it cannot understand. A **rational soul** is animated only by the human spirit, and as we shall see in the next chapter, is limited to understanding intangible material realities.

In contrast, **souls** are animated by the spirit of faith, which allows for the understanding of intangible spiritual realities. Such souls can understand and perceive the realities of the next world, a purely spiritual world, and can therefore use their free will to advance.

Possessed of this knowledge now we can understand the following question and answer:

Question: Through what means will the spirit of man – that is to say, the **rational soul** – after departing from this mortal world, make progress?

Answer: The progress of man's spirit in the divine world, after the severance of its connection with the body of dust, is through the bounty and grace of the Lord alone, or through the intercession and the sincere prayers of other human souls, or through the charities and important good works which are performed in its name. [23]

Because the difference between a soul and a rational soul was not understood, the question and answer were not understood, which gave rise to a widespread misunderstanding of the role of free will in the next world. This is why 'Abdu'l-Bahá's admonition that we take responsibility for the investigation of reality is so important. Remember, the principle is the **independent** investigation of reality.

Lest we imagine that conceptual thinking is a new principle, let's read this ancient parable that teaches the danger of making a premature leap from a fact to a concept:

Three blind men stand on the side of the road when they hear and feel the approach of a large animal. The three men begin to touch and explore the animal with their hands as it passes by. The first man grasps the tail and pronounces the unseen animal to be a snake-like creature. The next blind man pats the tusk and declares the animal to be as hard and smooth as a polished stone. The third rests his hand on the broad, fanning ear and declares that any animal with such a 'wing' must be some sort of large bird. Each of the blind men knows a real fact about the elephant and, on the basis of that single fact alone, proceeds to form an erroneous concept.

Sadly, humanity is acting like the three blind men by failing to perceive the underlying oneness of the world's religions that are like rivers flowing from the same source.

In the next and final chapter, we explore how only the spiritual nature possesses the sight to actually see the material and spiritual aspects of reality, which is the necessary prerequisite for the independent investigation of reality. In other words, we have to see reality before we can investigate reality, and only our spiritual nature possesses that capacity. Then and only then are we in a position to give and receive genuine acts of service that produce spiritual transformation.

The Options Chart

Facet to be considered in determining an act of service	Optional	Not Optional	Chapter
Must use our mind, animated by the spirit of faith, to make divinely principled choices that help bring us and others closer to God.		X	9

The whole, completed Options Chart can be found in appendix 1.

SECTION FOUR

As it describes the roles and relationships of our three natures – animal, human and spiritual – this section's single chapter focuses, in particular, on the purpose and power of our spiritual nature.

> The oneness of humankind is the pivotal principle and ultimate goal of His mission. This principle means far more than the reawakening of the spirit of brotherhood and goodwill among people: 'It implies an organic change in the structure of present-day society, a change such as the world has not yet experienced.' The Covenant of Bahá'u'lláh embodies the spirit, instrumentality and method to attain this essential goal. In addition to laying down, in His Book of Laws, the fundamentals for a new World Order, Bahá'u'lláh, in the Book of His Covenant, confirmed the appointment of His Son 'Abdu'l-Bahá as the interpreter of His Word and the Centre of His Covenant. As the interpreter, 'Abdu'l-Bahá became the living mouth of the Book, the expounder of the Word; as the Centre of the Covenant, He became the incorruptible medium for applying the Word to practical measures for the raising up of a new civilization. The Covenant is, therefore, unique as a divine phenomenon, in that Bahá'u'lláh, further to conferring upon 'Abdu'l-Bahá the necessary authority to fulfil the requirements of His singular office, vested in Him the virtues of perfection in personal and social behaviour, that humanity may have an enduring model to emulate. In no annals of the past is there recorded such an arrangement for ensuring the realization of the purpose of the Manifestation of God.[1]

Humanity has been summoned by Bahá'u'lláh, as a part of its coming of age, into the highest possibilities for which it has been created, to undergo an organic change at the deepest possible level reflected in the 'everyday behaviour' of human beings. Such an organic change is not only possible – it is inevitable.

Each one of us must summon our own better angels in the form of our spiritual nature – the only part of us that can touch 'the hem of the robe to which have clung all in this world and in the world to come'.[2]

Again, the guidance offered by the Universal House of Justice in its 1974 letter on material suffering seems to point towards essential components in the unfoldment of that organic process:

1) They need to know who they are.

2) They need to know to what purpose they exist.

3) They need to know how they should act towards one another.

4) **They need to be helped to gradually apply these answers to everyday behaviour.**

COMING HOME TO OUR SPIRITUAL NATURE

The holy Manifestations of God come into the world to dispel the darkness of the animal, or physical, nature of man, to purify him from his imperfections in order that his heavenly and spiritual nature may become quickened, his divine qualities awakened, his perfections visible, his potential powers revealed and all the virtues of the world of humanity latent within him may come to life.[3]

If, on the contrary, the spiritual nature of the soul has been so strengthened that it holds the material side in subjection, then does the man approach the Divine; his humanity becomes so glorified that the virtues of the Celestial Assembly are manifested in him; he radiates the Mercy of God, he stimulates the spiritual progress of mankind, for he becomes a lamp to show light on their path.[4]

The authors' intention in assembling this book is to encourage all of us to investigate our own reality and to use that knowledge to make better decisions, build life-affirming relationships and help bring forth beneficial results in our own lives and in the world.

What we have learned in the previous chapters has, hopefully, made it somewhat easier for one individual to treat another as one servant of God serving another servant of God. The spiritual nature, the highest part of us, will never be content with a lesser standard of behaviour. The great gift that Bahá'u'lláh has given us in this age is that we can, by how we treat each other, alleviate human suffering.

In the same 1974 letter that has served as an outline for this book the Universal House of Justice has written:

The principal cause of this suffering, which one can witness wherever one turns, is the corruption of human morals and the prevalence of prejudice, suspicion, hatred, untrustworthiness, selfishness and tyranny among men.[5]

One inevitable outcome of investigating reality is an increase in happiness and a decrease in suffering, not only for each of us as individuals, but for the world. The guidance in the 1974 letter of the Universal House of Justice links the unbalanced and misdirected inner state of individuals with the material suffering of humanity.

Yet 'Abdu'l-Bahá tells us in the above quotations that if our spiritual nature becomes the prevailing influence in our life, we 'approach the Divine' and stimulate 'the spiritual progress of mankind'.[6]

In light of that, it may be helpful to think of the first nine chapters of this book as something similar to the information required to build a state-of-the-art automobile. Chapter by chapter, segment by segment, a magnificent vehicle slowly takes form, until at last all the parts are assembled.

The question then becomes: 'Where is the driver who has the capacity and skill to draw on the full potential of this vehicle?' No matter how perfect the automobile, it will go nowhere if there is no qualified driver or, worse, an incompetent driver who will get behind the wheel and cause damage to the car and/or to other vehicles.

Both a car and a human life require a competent operator, and the authors suggest that it is our spiritual nature that is designed to be that driver in our lives. This nature is the aspect of ourselves that can embody the widest kind of vision. It is also the one that has the capacity to answer those four vital questions posed by the Universal House of Justice in its 1974 letter, which links the terrible material suffering of humanity with ignorance (ignoring) of the human reality.

The first three of those questions delineate three essential understandings that the human soul requires. The fourth describes what can then flow naturally from those understandings. That is, once we, as a soul, understand our true identity, our purpose and how it is that we are created to act towards one another, we can be 'helped to gradually apply these answers to everyday behaviour', i.e. to apply this essential knowledge of our true selves in order to become a truly well-trained driver of the vehicle entrusted to us. And it is a very great and wondrous trust, one that can, ultimately, if mysteriously, lead us to 'approach the Divine', what is of God.

Before we begin an explanation of the various natures of a human being, it is helpful to know that while a number of the passages from the Bahá'í writings describe two natures, 'Abdu'l-Bahá has elsewhere described three:

> Therefore we say that man is a reality which stands between light and darkness. From this standpoint of view, his nature is threefold, animal, human and divine. The animal nature is darkness; the heavenly is light in light.[7]

> ... in the microcosm there are deposited three realities ... an outer or physical reality ... a second reality, the rational or intellectual reality; and ... a third reality ... the spiritual reality.[8]

Do We Have More Than One Self?

First concerning the human soul and its nature. According to the Bahá'í conception, the soul of man, or in other words his inner spiritual self or reality, is not dualistic. There is no such thing, as the Zoroastrians believe, as a double reality in man, a definite higher self and lower self. The latter is capable of development in either way. All depends fundamentally on the training or education which man receives. **Human nature** is made up of possibilities for both good and evil. True religion can enable it to soar in the highest realm of the spirit, while its absence can, as we already witness around us, cause it to fall to the lowest depth of degradation and misery.[9]

'Satan' or 'satanic' are terms associated with the lower nature and do not refer to an evil entity.

> The reality underlying this question is that the evil spirit, Satan or whatever is interpreted as evil, refers to the lower nature of man ... God has never created an evil spirit ...[10]

> But the spirit of man has two aspects: one divine, one **satanic** – that is to say, it is capable of the utmost perfection, or it is capable of the

utmost **imperfection**. If it acquires virtues, it is the most noble of the existing beings; and if it acquires vices, it becomes the most degraded existence.[11]

Note that in the above passage 'satanic' is a synonym for imperfection.

... Satan being a product of human minds and of instinctive human tendencies toward error. God alone is Creator, and all are creatures of His might.[12]

Is there a part of us that is innately evil?
Then it is proved that there is no evil in existence; all that God created He created good.[13]

Then what, exactly, is evil?

'Abdu'l-Bahá said that 'Evil is imperfection.'[14]

He expands on this statement in the chapter on 'The Nonexistence of Evil' in *Some Answered Questions*,[15] stating 'blindness [imperfection] is the want of sight [perfection]' and that 'stupidity is the want of good sense'.

It gets complicated when He goes on to explain, 'Nevertheless a doubt occurs to the mind – that is, scorpions and serpents are poisonous. Are they good or evil, for they are existing beings? Yes, a scorpion is evil in **relation** to man; but in relation to themselves they are not evil ...'

It is this last part of 'Abdu'l-Bahá's explanation that we want to keep in mind when we read the descriptions of our various natures. The key word is **relationship**. A proper relationship between the animal, human and spiritual natures means that the contributions of each of these natures are valuable and to be valued.

Yet it is our spiritual nature that is best equipped to maximize the purpose of our free will by choosing effective and beneficial decisions – ones that are in harmony with our true identity and purpose. However, the greatest possibility for this exists when our three natures, rather than acting as contenders or separate entities, are related in harmony (even as the Universal House of Justice reminds us in its 1974 letter that the outward disunity and suffering of humanity reflect the inner state of individuals).

So, if there is no evil demon lurking inside us and there is no innately evil nature, then how is it possible that human beings are capable of evil actions?

The answer can be found in one of the premises that we focused on in the last chapter about the mind – namely, that all meaning is found within the context of the ever-evolving, eternal Covenant of God. The moral worth of all tangible and intangible realities and the moral worth of all actions are determined by the parameters of the Covenant established by the Manifestation of God. Therefore the proper relationship between the animal, human and spiritual natures is determined by this as well.

But how can these very different natures of a human being work together in harmony? Don't they want different things? Don't they have different goals?

It only appears that way on the surface when they are out of balance and acting outside of the Covenant. The three natures – indeed, every atom in existence, Bahá'u'lláh tells us – have the same goal, as described in the following quotation:

> The Creator of all is One God.
>
> From this same God all creation sprang into existence, and He is the **one goal**, towards which everything in nature yearns.[16]

Built into the essence of existence is an eternal, unquenchable desire to approach the Presence of God, which is translated into an eternal, unquenchable desire for perfection. This does not mean that everything in existence is aware of the true nature of its yearning for perfection, however. Only the spiritual nature has the capability of understanding that the desire for perfection is actually a desire to 'approach the Divine'.

Author John Hatcher explains this same concept in his book *Close Connections*:

> In other words, as emanations from God, we are fashioned so that we are, in truth, always seeking a single objective – proximity to God, however unaware we may be that all attraction we feel to **anything** and to **everything is but a veiled expression of or allusion to attaining the presence of God**.[17]

Let's approach this concept from an entirely different perspective and ask ourselves: Would a just and loving God who, we have been told, created us out of love for us, really design a human being in such a way as to ensure a perpetual state of inner war?

One measure we can use to gauge our success in reaching a state of balance and establishing a proper relationship between our three natures is that when we do, as the guidance in all of the world's spiritual teachings consistently promises, we will feel as though we are approaching a state of inner peace and harmony – approaching what is, verily, of God.

Animal Nature

What we describe here about the animal nature also holds true for human and spiritual natures. As each succeeding nature encompasses those that precede it, it thus possesses the qualities and kind of sight or perception that also belongs to those levels of animating spirit that comprise it.

> . . . and the animal spirit – in other words, the power of the senses – is produced. It will **perceive** the reality of things from that which is seen and visible, audible, edible, tangible and that which can be smelled.[18]

> Man is distinguished above the animals through his reason. The perceptions of man are of two kinds: tangible, or sensible, and reasonable, whereas the animal perceptions are limited to the senses, the tangible only.[19]

All three natures possess a type of perception. According to 'Abdu'l-Bahá's words above, the perceptions of the animal nature are limited to realities that can be perceived by the outer senses.

The perceptions of the human nature are limited to what the animal nature perceives plus the ability to see or comprehend intangible realities of the material world, such as abstract concepts.

Our spiritual nature sees the qualities of the realities of the material and spiritual world to the extent that we exist in the condition of servitude. And a being that exists in the higher condition of prophethood, such as a Christ or Buddha or Bahá'u'lláh, also beholds the essence of reality.

This relationship of the three natures and the levels of spirit and perception might become clearer in the form of a simple graph:

Nature	Animating Power	Perception	Example	Goal
Animal	Animal Spirit	tangible material realities	'chair'	perfection (God)
Human	Human Spirit	tangible material realities	'time'	perfection (God)
Spiritual	Spirit of Faith	tangible material realities	'relationships'	perfection/God

The senses of the animal nature and their corresponding perceptive abilities evolved over millions of years. This spirit-driven evolutionary process has been motivated by a built-in desire for survival, which is achieved by a never-ending quest for perfection. Obviously there is nothing evil about such a purpose. But information derived solely from our physical senses is often prone to error and, if acted upon, can result in harmful decisions.

Imagine that a small group of primitive hunters sees an animal approaching. The animal is a good distance away but coming toward them very quickly. The hunters confer together: if the beast is a leaf-eater, then it makes sense for them to stay and kill it because the animal is one gigantic meal for the tribe. If, on the other hand, it is a ferocious meat-eater and they wait too long to make a decision, they may become its dinner.

The hunters decide that their survival is at stake and they cannot take the chance of waiting until they know for sure what sort of creature is approaching. If our ancestors had behaved differently than this, we might not be having this discussion today.

In his book *The Emotional Brain*, neuroscientist Dr Joseph LeDoux offers the example of walking on a path in the woods and seeing a curled stick blocking the way. Or is it a stick? Maybe it is a cleverly camouflaged poisonous snake. Most people calculate that it is safer to give the suspicious object a wide berth. LeDoux says, 'You are better off mistaking a stick for a snake than a snake for a stick.'[20] He is emphasizing that having a very rapid – if imprecise – method of detecting danger is of high survival value.

Here is a diagram showing how, in the emotional brain, accuracy is sacrificed for speed:

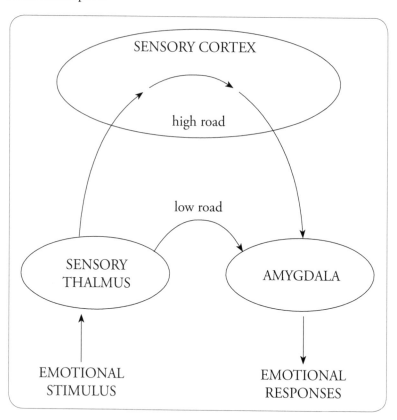

Based on LeDoux, *The Emotional Brain*, p. 164

First, some definitions for some of the terms used above would be helpful. The amygdala is an almond-shaped structure in the brain (we actually have two of them, located in the frontal portion of our brain's temporal lobe). It is essential to our ability to feel certain emotions, such as fear, and to perceive them in others. If we're being followed at night, our amygdala is probably very active. The amygdala allows us to react almost instantaneously to the presence of a danger, so quickly that we may startle first, then realize only later what it was that frightened us.

All information perceived by our outer senses is first routed through our sensory thalamus. The job of the thalamus is to send the message to the appropriate part of our brain's sensory cortex (visual, auditory, etc.), which assesses and assigns meaning to the incoming information. If the information is deemed threatening, the sensory cortex then informs the amygdala, which triggers the appropriate emotional response.

It has recently been discovered, however, that in some instances the information received by the thalamus is transferred directly to the amygdala, without even passing through the sensory cortex at all. This is the rapid reaction behind our natural, survival-focused alarm system. The incoming information that travels this 'low road' from the sensory thalamus directly to the amygdala moves twice as quickly as the information that travels the high road from the sensory thalamus to the sensory cortex to the amygdala. There is a trade-off in terms of the quality of information that travels on this low road from the sensory thalamus to the amygdala in a perception of potential threat. In exchange for speed, the information is crude and incomplete.

In the first example, the hunters were acting on the faster, albeit sketchy, information that travels the low road because the slightest delay could mean the difference between life and death. Millions of years later, that low-road pathway still exists in our brains. We can dress in fine clothes, be well-groomed, earn numerous degrees but we can also still make incredibly quick decisions on a small amount of what is often inaccurate information. A primitive part of us is still asking the same question over and over in its interactions with the world: 'Do I eat it or does it eat me?'

Animal Nature and Blind Imitation

In the beginning chapters we focused on numerous quotations from the Bahá'í writings that describe how the evil in the world comes into existence because of blind imitation. Such blind imitation undoubtedly has its roots in a very old evolutionary system whose purpose is to ensure physical survival.

Problems arise when our primitive emotional brain is still sending out signals warning of charging beasts and snakes that look like sticks when the current-day 'threats' are simply others who are unknown to us or may appear or think differently. The more different they are from us, the greater the perceived threat to our survival. People of different nationalities, races, thought processes or belief systems represent the unknown, and any unknown is seen as a possible threat, which prompts the animal nature to send out a fight-or-flight signal.

If we are seeing only with the perception of our animal nature, we are assessing a situation based solely on outer appearances. While some strangers may present a danger, an investigation of the reality of the situation is required to see whether there truly is danger or not. If there is no investigation of reality, blind imitation flourishes.

In chapter 2, which addressed blind imitation, 'Abdu'l-Bahá was quoted as saying, 'the root cause of prejudice is blind imitation'.[21] A workable definition of prejudice is that it is an emotional commitment to ignorance. The primitive hunter might demonstrate an emotional commitment to ignorance when faced with a charging beast. This prejudice of our primitive ancestors allowed them to survive but blindly following that same fight-or-flight signal today perpetuates racism and oppression, destroys families and societies, causes wars and prevents the realization of the oneness of humanity.

Closely related to the concept of the unknown is the concept of change. Change implies moving from the known to the unknown. A curled stick that might be a snake represents a worrisome change in the physical environment. It is a suspicious imperfection blocking the path. This imperfection can be eliminated by throwing a big rock at the snake or the stick – the primitive hunter didn't care which it really was, because he simply crushed it or chased it away. This is how our distant ancestors handled imperfection.

The problem is that what was successful behaviour for our ancient relatives is a disaster when applied in most present-day situations and interactions. Throwing big rocks or running away from the unknown, or imperfection or change, doesn't solve a problem; it only makes it worse. Relationships are destroyed when we follow this course of action. Spouses, children, friends, business associates and even total strangers don't appreciate having 'big rocks' thrown at them.

Another serious danger occurs when this imperfection-seeing eye is trained inward. The individual becomes the imperfection that needs to be destroyed. At the very least there is a loss of self-esteem but the worst-case scenario entails self-loathing, self-destructive behaviour and even suicide – all of which, the principle of oneness tells us, brings damage not just to individuals but to us all.

The unknown and imperfection are always regarded as threats to survival, and threats to survival generate a fight-or-flight signal from the animal nature. It's obvious that if we are ruled solely by the powerful survival signals of the animal nature, there is no escaping the death grip of blind imitation. And it is blind imitation that we know to be at the root of our most intractable problems.

Fortunately we do possess a higher nature, which is capable of accepting the beneficial, legitimate survival signals of the animal nature while also possessing the wisdom to reject the illegitimate and harmful signals the animal nature generates. We will learn more about the spiritual nature on the following pages but let's remember that all three of our natures have the same goal. A yearning for what is of God is expressed in the common striving of all three natures for perfection but only the spiritual nature possesses the level of perception to realize that the yearning is a desire to 'approach the Divine'.

Human Nature

> The human spirit consists of the rational, or logical, reasoning faculty, which apprehends general ideas and things intelligible and perceptible.[22]

> But the mind is the power of the human spirit. Spirit is the lamp; mind is the light which shines from the lamp. Spirit is the tree, and the mind is the fruit. Mind is the perfection of the spirit, and is its essential quality, as the sun's rays are the essential necessity of the sun.[23]

Nature	Animating Power	Perception	Example	Goal
Human	Human Spirit	tangible material realities	'time'	perfection (God)

In the first passage quoted above, 'Abdu'l-Bahá characterizes the human spirit, which animates our human nature, as our rational, or logical, reasoning. Since the human nature encompasses the animal nature, it has access to the powers of that nature, yet its own powers can challenge the signals generated by the animal nature. In the chart above, we have chosen as an example the intangible reality of 'time' in order to focus on just how the human nature can override the reactions of the animal nature.

Say that one person had a distressing confrontation with another and was filled with powerful emotions of anger and animosity in that encounter. Five years later the two people meet again. Again the individual is flooded with exactly the same set of terrible emotions. As far as that person's primitive emotional brain is concerned, it is as if no time had passed.

Now let us imagine a scenario in which a woman is about to give birth to twins. She is shocked to discover that a doctor who had made a critical mistake that came close to damaging her newborn years earlier has recently rejoined her medical group and will very likely be a part of her delivery team. The doctor's previous mistake didn't harm her child, but she still feels angry about what happened.

Then her husband asks a question that reflects the role that time may have played in the interim: 'How do we know that this doctor hasn't changed in the years that have passed? He may be worse, he may be better, but we just don't know and to be fair we need to find out.'

They make an appointment with the doctor and he expresses remorse for his past mistake and his youthful arrogance, and he tells the couple that the mistake prompted him to return to school and to rededicate his life to being the very best doctor he could be. He also demonstrates a newfound humility and compassion.

Because the couple was willing to make an independent investigation of reality, they overcame the powerful forces of blind imitation.

Now, we are not saying that it was wrong for the animal nature to send those signals in the first place. It was, in itself, an important warning sign that the mother and the child could be in danger. The animal nature simply fulfilled its function but then the human nature did, too, as it contributed its more expansive information in the light of what the passage of time could reveal and unfold.

All three natures share the same goal of moving towards perfection, and this is particularly apparent with regard to the human nature. Most work situations involve recognizing a problem and resolving it and this is what the human nature excels at. What usually happens is that an imperfection is perceived and the human nature, using the power of the rational mind, figures out a way to achieve perfection, or at least correction. A plumber repairs a leaky pipe, an editor corrects a grammatically faulty sentence, or a carpenter repairs a broken fence. This is what the human nature, with the aid of the mental faculties, is well-suited to accomplish.

The difficulty arises when, after solving problems all day at work, we return home and treat family and others we know as 'problems' to be solved, as imperfections. Left unchallenged, the limited perception of the human nature will opt to fix, destroy or run away from the imperfection it perceives, wherever it perceives it.

While the animal nature's response is to simply put some physical distance between itself and the perceived threat that it sees in all imperfection, or to fight it off as needed, the human nature can also choose to fight or 'run away" emotionally from the situation. Most often, it may choose to 'run away' by using drugs and alcohol, or other means of withdrawal and escape, and this alienating behaviour can destroy relationships.

In sum, the human nature is great at completing tasks and solving physical problems but is incapable of sustaining relationships on its own, or even of developing true understanding about the individual's own life. It is this nature that often invests great energy in trying to protect or seek advantage for erroneous notions that it holds to be true about itself. These are those very idle fancies and vain imaginings, activities of the insistent self, that Bahá'u'lláh warns us about so repeatedly. Preoccupation with these, unaccompanied by a growing sense of true spiritual identity and investigation of reality, lead inevitably to increased suffering and confusion, a form of blind imitation practised at the personal level.

The abilities of the animal and human natures are a double-edged sword, it seems, that can be used to help or harm. The logical course of action is to employ the wisdom of our spiritual nature to accept what is a genuinely helpful contribution from these aspects of ourselves, leave what is potentially harmful and thus claim true responsibility for reality-inspired participation in and stewardship of our own life.

Spiritual Nature

But the human spirit, unless assisted by the spirit of faith, does not become acquainted with the **divine secrets** and **heavenly realities**.[24]

Nature	Animating Power	Perception	Example	Goal
Spiritual	Spirit of Faith	tangible material realities	'relationships'	Perfection/God

In the illustration above, the word 'perfection', also the goal for the animal and human natures, is now capitalized. This represents the higher level of perception of the spiritual nature, which understands through inner wisdom and the spirit of faith that the shared goal of perfection possessed by all three of our natures is really a yearning for what is of God.

In representing the spiritual nature in this chart, we have chosen human relationships for the example of an intangible spiritual reality. In chapter 7, 'The Spirit of Faith', we reflected on the reality that human beings are servants of God – and that we are 'divine secrets' and 'heavenly realities'. Therefore the relationships we form are also 'divine secrets' and 'heavenly realities' and as such cannot be adequately understood by our lower natures.

Years ago, Ron climbed into his car to go to work one day only to find that his keys weren't where he customarily left them, in the vehicle's ignition. To his surprise, not only were his keys missing but his wife Karen's car was as well.

This had happened before and Ron assumed that Karen had once again taken his keys in a hurried panic because her car key was on his key chain and she'd been running late for work.

He sat on his front porch, fuming and furious. She had undoubtedly thought he had another key, as he'd been talking about getting some duplicates made. But he did not. Right then, the missing key was his number one and seemingly only focus and it was stirring up a lot of negative feelings.

Then another voice came into his awareness and he began to laugh, and this also helped him to calm down rather quickly. That voice asked which of his natures it was that was causing his ire and whether he really valued a two-dollar key over the wife he loved and had shared his life with for so long.

He also put the powers of his human nature to work the next day and went to the hardware store to finally have some extra keys made.

As a young mother Phyllis encountered many experiences that reflected the struggle we can have until our natures begin collaborating in harmony and our spiritual nature helps to put first things first. One afternoon she was waiting for a call-back from the editor of a large magazine about whether he would use an article she had submitted that he'd kept for a long time. She was anxious about what his verdict would be and tried to keep her mind and attention busy preparing dinner.

Her young son, then five, kept asking to help with things she was doing in the kitchen but she only shooed him off, telling him, 'No, not now. Mommy's busy.'

Then the phone rang. As she watched in disbelief, her son raced toward it, grabbed up the receiver, and said cheerily, 'Hang up, willya?' then did exactly that.

Their eyes met in frozen silence before it rang again.

'You will sit over there and wait for me until I'm finished,' she told him, struggling to contain her anger.

Then she noticed the uncertain fear – and sadness – in his eyes. In that moment he looked very alone and very confused. He would later tell her, 'I wanted to help because you were so busy.'

Undoubtedly his intuitive nature and sensitivity had picked up her tense 'vibe' that afternoon and he truly wanted to offer help, something she had been steadily refusing.

On the second call the editor joked with her, 'After hanging up your manuscript so long, I probably deserved that.' He also asked good-naturedly after her small son and told her that the magazine was going to buy her article, her first major publication credit.

Afterwards, Phyllis wanted to call six friends to share this hoped-for news but her spiritual nature knew there was a far more important matter waiting at the kitchen table, where her son sat looking miserable. From his small perspective he'd made a brave attempt to do a helpful, grown-up thing and it had failed dismally.

The most significant thing Phyllis did that day, perhaps that year, was to acknowledge his intent, to thank him for it – and also to apologize for her own misunderstanding. They then talked about telephone courtesy and together, with pencil and crayons, crafted a note to send to the magazine editor, who replied to the young writer with a bright and friendly postcard a few days later.

The spiritual nature has a value system that places priceless relationships above any object or hoped-for outcome. But the human nature, if left in charge, does not.

All of us have no doubt found ourselves chagrined by our overreaction to a situation, as if our life were threatened when, in actuality, we have merely been inconvenienced. It helps to develop the habit of questioning ourselves: 'What is at stake here? What truly stands to be gained or lost? Is something in my life really being threatened or am I simply being inconvenienced? What am I not yet perceiving?'

The answers will show us how our various natures work. For Ron and Phyllis, in each of these situations the human nature perceived an imperfection and that information was shared with both the animal nature and the spiritual nature.

The animal nature, with its primitive emotional brain, sees all threats as life-or-death. There is no reflection on this level – no nuances or grey areas – and the signals it sends out are powerful. If these signals aren't challenged, the rational mind of the human nature will be overpowered, resulting in potential damage to the fragile balance in relationships.

On the other hand, if the spiritual nature receives the information from the human nature that an imperfection exists and then challenges whether it is a life-threatening situation, the spiritual nature can then respond by choosing an act of service guided by its perception of spiritual reality to solve the problem, unencumbered by destructive negative qualities.

This, by the way, is how we know that it is the spiritual nature making the decisions: it will always see the underlying spiritual reality of any material situation and choose an act of service based on that heightened level of perception.

In Ron's case, it chose love and forgiveness, then empowered his human, problem-solving nature towards a practical step that would benefit the members of his household. In Phyllis's case, response began with seeing the spiritual nobility of another and responding to it, telling the truth about her own behaviour, then receiving the situation as a learning opportunity for all involved.

When 'Abdu'l-Bahá visited New York City in 1912, He gave one of the most moving talks to an assembled group of the downtrodden and homeless at a mission in the Bowery district. He began by saying:

> Tonight I am very happy, for I have come here to meet my friends. I consider you relatives, my companions; and I am your comrade.[25]

He went on to compare these men to Jesus, who, He said, 'had no place to lay His head, no home. He was exposed in the open to heat, cold and frost . . .'[26]

When we turn to and rely upon the vision of our spiritual nature, we discover a similar, compassionate vision of all souls as servants of God possessed of innate honour and nobility, sharing the same essential circumstances and challenges. When this kind of vision inspires heartfelt and genuine acts of service, these act as catalysts in the establishment of what's so often called the Kingdom of God, right here on earth.

The sign that we're in a situation that requires a shift from the eyes of our human nature to the vision of our spiritual one is when we find ourselves focusing on the imperfections of others to such an extent that we experience an increasing intensity of negative emotions that, in turn, causes deterioration in personal relationships.

The only escape from this vicious cycle is to change what we see and elevate our perception and to begin looking at others with the sin (imperfection)-covering eye of the spiritual nature.

The spiritual nature doesn't dwell on perceived imperfections but instead seeks the missing spiritual attributes that the situation is calling for and creates an act of service designed to release those latent virtues, which exist within the heart of every servant of God. When that happens, the destructive negative emotions and imperfections begin to dissipate. They are, after all, merely perceptions and 'decisions' of the mind or human nature, and the resulting emotion is the energy of those thoughts in motion.

However, in the survival-motivated blind imitation that is the lower nature's customary behaviour, our mind and emotions can liken the current experience to one that has registered as negative in the past. In order to truly investigate the reality of the matter, we need the spiritual nature and its vision to come into the driver's seat, to interrupt this reflexive imitating of what happened – or what we perceive to have happened – in the past. If we are unwilling to do this, we will remain prisoners of that past, and of what, in essence, is actually an imagined past, the perspective of the mind alone.

A sign that we're progressing away from imitation towards investigation is that negative emotions are replaced by positive ones and there is also a noticeable improvement both in the way we ourselves feel and within the tone of the relationship.

Spirit, the power that animates all life, generates different levels of perception.

> The greatest power in the realm and range of human existence is spirit – the divine breath which animates and pervades all things. It is manifested throughout creation in different degrees or kingdoms.[27]

Different degrees of spirit generate different levels of perception and awareness. Imagine the soul is a large, three-story house. Now imagine walking up to the front door of this large house. It is a dark night and the house is also dark inside. We open the front door and switch on the light.

The animal spirit provides the light for the first floor and what is seen is the 'visible, audible, edible, tangible and that which can be smelled'. We walk over to the window and look out and see part of the front lawn but our vision is blocked by a large wooden fence.

We continue exploring the house and walk up the stairs to the second floor. We open the door and switch on the light. The human spirit provides the light for the second floor. It enables us to engage our 'rational, or logical, reasoning faculty, which apprehends general ideas and things intelligible and perceptible'. On this floor it is possible to see the abstract mysteries of the physical universe. We again walk over to a window and see the front lawn and the wooden fence, and a little farther beyond it, to where our vision is blocked by a stand of tall trees.

We continue up to the third floor and switch on the light there. The spirit of faith provides the light this time and what we can see are the 'divine secrets and heavenly realities'. A spiritual universe is waiting to be explored here, and as we look out of the window, we see the front lawn, over and past the large fence and far beyond the tall trees.

As we climb higher in the house, the scope of our vision becomes more encompassing and as we learn to see more with the eye of the spiritual nature, we are able to see both material and spiritual realities.

Let's look again at a passage that suggests that all three of our natures strive for the same goal of perfection, thereby making it possible for these natures to achieve a harmonious unity:

> The Creator of all is One God.
> From this same God all creation sprang into existence, and He is the one goal, towards which everything in nature yearns.[28]

If we consider that the 'one goal', or God, is the same as Perfection, we can also see that the infinite attributes of God manifested in the animal, human and spiritual realms are a reflection of that Perfection. For example, Bahá'í prayers typically conclude by calling to awareness attributes of God such as the 'Giver, the All-Bountiful'. Such generosity is reflected in all that God has created, yet our understanding of this, or any other attribute of God, is limited by the capacity and perception of our animal, human and spiritual natures.

The most subtle and most difficult transition for us to make is to move from the use and understanding of human traits by the human nature to the employing of the qualities or attributes of God by the spiritual nature. This has been described as the longest journey – from the mind to the heart.

The human nature, using the limited vision of the rational mind, doesn't have the capacity to perceive divinity and easily makes the mistake of believing that we, ourselves, are the source of such spiritually motivated actions as generosity, mercy and justice. This misconception leads inevitably to arrogance, the hallmark of the ego, and we cannot approach God with what is essentially the exact opposite of the attribute that is required for this – humility.

In his book *Love, Power and Justice* author William Hatcher notes that 'we are the only creatures of God who have the capacity to be aware of our dependency on God'. He goes on to say,

> This, then, gives us the fundamental moral principle governing our relationship with God: In relationship to God, whatever increases our awareness of our dependency on Him is good, and whatever hides or veils from us the knowledge of the ways we are dependent on Him is bad.[29]

It is the spiritual nature that possesses the capacity to recognize that these amazing virtues of love, mercy, kindness originate with God and that we are privileged to use these infinite attributes that God has placed within us in infinite combinations to enhance our lives. We can remember now, when someone thanks us for being kind or merciful, to acknowledge in our heart the divine source of kindness or mercy. In this way we can grow in humility instead of in arrogance. We can carry in our awareness the source of these qualities and thus draw closer to that source.

The animal and human nature each ask the same question in all our interactions with the world: 'Do I eat it or does it eat me?' The human nature wears better clothes and couches the same question in more sophisticated language, such as, 'Do I win or do you win?' or 'Who controls whom in this relationship?'

The spiritual nature always asks the same question, no matter in what world it happens to reside: 'What do I need to do to "approach the Divine"?' Or perhaps more specifically: 'What act of service do I need to give or receive in order to "approach the Divine"?'

And again, the two service questions are tools we can use as we ask this:

1) At this moment in time, what is the act of service I am capable of giving that the other person is capable of receiving?

2) At this moment in time, what is the act of service I am capable of receiving that the other person is capable of giving?

The wisdom of the spiritual nature enables it to accept the worthwhile contributions of the human and animal natures while rejecting any harmful influence their perceptions might bring with them. The spiritual nature can also use the full potential of all our powers and faculties, known and unknown, to create unique acts of service, either giving or receiving, that respond to and address those important understandings:

1) Who we are

2) To what purpose we exist

3) How we should act towards one another

4) And help us gradually apply these answers to everyday behaviour.

What the Universal House of Justice also emphasized in that 1974 letter is that these essentials are what the people of the world, each and every one of us, **desperately** need to know. A word like 'desperate' might bring to mind individuals wandering in the desert, an image Bahá'u'lláh used quite frequently when referring to the plight of humanity, and of the individual soul that does not understand who it is and for what purpose it exists.

Imagine we are such desert-bound souls desperately seeking water. If we are offered anything but water we will turn away. We might be offered a change of clothes, food, shelter – all good things. But the desperate nature of life-threatening thirst will cause the thirsty one to reject what is offered as if the offering were poison.

When we experience intense suffering personally, our world seems to narrow dramatically and become very small. Imagine the intense pain we feel when we sustain a deep burn or when we sustain a loss. Do we really care at that moment about any other needs in our life, no matter how legitimate they are? The need that seems most desperate can crowd out of our consciousness all other needs until that need is met, whether it is removing our hand from a heat source, healing from grief or quenching our thirst with life-giving water.

If it is our desperate need to discover our authentic self and purpose, then once we know that true identity and purpose and understand the most beneficial ways to act, we'll be ready for other things.

A father held up in front of his teenage daughter a brightly-coloured box with eye-catching ribbons and bells.

When the daughter asked what it was, her father replied, 'Look how nicely the box is wrapped!'

With more edge in her voice, the young woman said, 'I see that! But what is it?'

Her father continued to respond to her questions by directing her attention to the package's wrapping until she grew angry and demanded to know what was in the box.

'If you become this frustrated this quickly when you aren't told the true identity and purpose of this silly box, just how much might you suffer if you were denied knowledge of your true identity and purpose?' he observed.

'Desperate' is undoubtedly a word that would apply. And then, eventually, perhaps hopeless, as well.

Without the awareness and involvement of our spiritual nature – who we truly are – our life is rather like a gift we can never unwrap nor fully receive.

How do we know when our spiritual nature is the prevailing influence in our life?

We have already introduced in the chapters on purpose and the mind information on a thought process called conceptual thinking. This is as good a phrase as any but we suspect language is inadequate to describe the thought process of the spiritual nature. That being said, let's restate our working definition of conceptual thinking:

> Conceptual thinking is the ability to identify patterns or connections between situations that are not obviously related and to identify key or underlying issues in complex situations. It includes using creative, conceptual or inductive reasoning.

This definition implies that the lower natures are capable of conceptual thinking and we agree. Wonderful out-of-the-box business solutions to complex problems emerge when the mind sees below the surface of '**situations that are not obviously related**' and that is valuable.

There is a story about P. T. Barnum of circus fame, who had a popular tent exhibit that was so captivating that spectators would enter and were then reluctant to leave. The ever-innovative Barnum came up with an ingenious solution. He posted a sign over the flap at the back of the tent that said, 'This way to the Egress'. Curious customers wanted to see the next exhibit, the Egress, only to discover that 'Egress' meant exit.

Barnum connected what was 'not obviously related' – human curiosity, making a profit and how to get people to leave without making enemies of potential future customers. His human nature was able to perceive a level below the surface to find an unusual but effective solution.

The spiritual nature is capable of seeing at much deeper 'not obviously related' levels below the surface. Imagine two people in a relationship. One is male, 40 years old, very interested in sports and works as a lawyer. The other is female, aged 30, with no interest at all in sports and is a yoga and meditation teacher. They are in a happy long-term relationship, although on the surface they have nothing in common. The facts about them show no obvious connections. How could these two complex spiritual realities survive for one day if they relied on fact-based thinking? Their attention would likely focus only on how different they are.

The relationship needs, as all relationships do, to be sustained by qualities like caring and generosity. They may or may not label these as attributes of God. They may express them in acts of service that they may or may not label that way. Each of them possesses qualities that are expressed in a way that fills a deep need to be whole. The relationship can only be strengthened, made even more sustainable, if there is understanding of – and appreciation for – what's going on under the surface.

The spiritual nature has that capacity for understanding. It sees these qualities as attributes of God expressed in acts of service and recognizes that a relationship has been created, almost a third entity, which consists of accumulated acts of service, giving and receiving. This relationship resembles a wonderful pattern being woven like cloth on a daily basis, the texture and design growing ever more beautiful and complex as time goes by. When each of these souls contributes to this third entity, it is no longer simply a me-and-you situation. Instead, a 'we' emerges and they begin to see with the eye of oneness.

The eye of oneness is the sight of the spiritual nature that sees deep beneath the surface of seemingly unrelated facts. It sees that we are all servants of God who are all capable of reflecting the infinite attributes of God, both giving and receiving, and are progressing at different rates towards the Creator. The oneness of humankind is not a social goal to be achieved but a spiritual reality to be realized. The inherent limitations of the animal and human natures don't allow them to attain such a vision of life.

Note the word 'limitation' in the following passage from the Seven Valleys of Bahá'u'lláh:

After passing through the Valley of Knowledge, which is the last plane of limitation, the wayfarer cometh to

The Valley of Unity

and drinketh from the cup of the Absolute, and gazeth on the Manifestations of Oneness. In this station he pierceth the veils of plurality, fleeth from the worlds of the flesh, and ascendeth into the heaven of singleness. With the ear of God he heareth, with the eye of God he beholdeth the mysteries of divine creation. He steppeth into the sanctuary of the Friend, and shareth as an intimate the pavilion of the Loved One . . . He looketh on all things with the eye of oneness, and seeth the brilliant rays of the divine sun shining from the dawning-point of Essence alike on all created things, and the lights of singleness reflected over all creation.[30]

Consider that the Valley of Knowledge is about the limitations of the human nature, whose main faculty is the mind, animated by the human spirit, and you are now about to enter the Valley of Unity. The mind then becomes empowered by the spirit of faith, which enables the spiritual nature to pierce '**the veils of plurality**' empowering the individual to see with '**the eye of oneness**'. Consider that you are now seeing with the eye of the spiritual nature and are seeing connections at the deepest level possible for a human being. You are now residing in a place of absolute safety: '**He steppeth into the sanctuary of the Friend.**'

And in the Hidden Word 'O Son of Being! Thy heart is My home; sanctify it for My descent. Thy spirit is My place of revelation; cleanse it for My manifestation',[31] Bahá'u'lláh may be describing the ultimate depth of vision possible for a human being guided by the spiritual nature, whose thinking process is conceptual in nature and whose instinctual reactions are acts of service.

Eventually we will see that everything in existence is connected and we have entered our true 'home'. Conceptual thinking and the increase of the presence and influence of the spiritual nature is the way of our future. Concept-based thinking leads to the investigation of reality and spiritual transformation, while reliance only on fact-based thinking can lead to blind imitation, perceived separation and fundamentalism.

Bahá'u'lláh, in the following quotation, makes a connection between justice, the eye of oneness and the removal of imitation – three things that may not, at first glance, seem to be 'obviously related':

> The essence of all that We have revealed for thee is **Justice**, is for man to free himself from idle fancy and **imitation**, discern with the **eye of oneness** His glorious handiwork, and look into all things with a searching eye.[32]

Simply stated, the thought process of the spiritual nature is conceptual in nature. Its perception is the eye of oneness that focuses on the 'building of the good' rather than on 'fighting evil' in every interaction. Its instinctual reaction is an act of service, either giving or receiving, which it arrives at by first determining what attribute of God is the motivating force behind that act of service. The bulk of its time is spent in contemplation of the needed divine quality, whether it is love, mercy, forgiveness, generosity, etc., and when clarity emerges as a result of the meditative process, the hard work has already been done. What remains is the outward act of service that embodies and conveys the attribute of God.

When the authors introduce the two service questions in workshops and classes, there is often confusion initially about how to use them because the all-important first step of determining the needed attribute of God is overlooked. This is an indication that the ever-pragmatic human nature is attempting to answer the two service questions.

At first, conceptual thinking may seem a cumbersome process. It soon becomes second nature, however, because we're simply learning how to live from a completely natural process that is in harmony with our true identity and purpose: that of a servant of God, patterned after the example of 'Abdu'l-Bahá.

Here are some ways we can know that it is our spiritual nature that is responding in any given circumstance:

1) In its inherent love and true humility, the spiritual nature considers what spiritual principles and elements of the Covenant of God would provide guidance in determining the appropriateness of any action, ideally an act of service, in any given situation.

2) The spiritual nature is the one nature capable of uniting all three natures, thus preventing a perpetual inner war, which significantly reduces destructive stress.

3) The spiritual nature is capable of transcending the level of perception that dwells on imperfection. It sees the imperfection but also sees the latent perfection in every situation and in every person. It directs all the energy of the individual into acts of service that build the good instead of fighting evil (imperfection). The eye of perfection of the spiritual nature is a 'sin-covering eye'.

4) The spiritual nature is capable of understanding that every genuine act of service moves the giver and receiver towards God and that acts of service are about more than simply solving material problems.

5) The spiritual nature accepts the contribution of the mind but knows that the heart, which contains 'the wellspring of divine treasures'[33] has the potential to create the most powerful and effective acts of service.

6) If the phone rings at 3:00 a.m. and we are asked who we are and our reply is, 'I am a servant of God', then the spiritual nature has certainly answered the phone.

It is the spiritual nature that has the ability to gather all the resources and knowledge from all our physical and spiritual powers and faculties – known and unknown – and guide us on an infinite, step-by-step journey into manifesting our unique identity and purpose. With the foundation of that awareness in place, we're then prepared, with the ongoing guidance of our spiritual nature, to grow into understanding just how it is we are to act on a day-by-day basis to satisfy that yearning of each of our three natures: to draw closer to Perfection, to that which is of God.

One noteworthy example of applying conceptual thinking to the sacred writings was the development, over a span of nearly 30 years, of a unique index of the Bahá'í writings. Through careful and thorough study of the writings, categories of being or existence were identified and the possible ways in which all these categories can be related to each other were documented. Once this was complete, indexers were trained to understand and make use of this categorization structure. All the writings of Bahá'u'lláh that had already been translated into English at the time were then meticulously indexed, page by page, paragraph by paragraph, by these volunteer indexers according to this categorization system. This 'Worlds of God Index' – comprising approximately 230,000 index cards that have since been computerized – is now a private project under the direction of J. Michael Kafes. More information is available at the website: www.worldsofgodindex.com.

The Heart and the Spiritual Nature

Of all the words that occur within the Word of God in the sacred writings of so many faiths perhaps one of the most beautiful and mysterious is 'heart'. Indeed, the following quotation identifies it as 'the dwelling of eternal mysteries'.

> O friend, **the heart is the dwelling of eternal mysteries**, make it not the home of fleeting fancies; waste not the treasure of thy precious life in employment with this swiftly passing world. Thou comest from the world of holiness – bind not thine heart to the earth; thou art a dweller in the court of nearness – choose not the homeland of dust.[34]

But the heart is also the home of our unique individual identity. In *Gate of the Heart*, author Nader Saiedi writes, 'The station of the heart is the highest stage of a created being's existential reality. It is the reflection of divine revelation itself within the inmost reality of things.'[35]

He goes on to emphasize that we become aware of what our heart contains when we accept the station of servitude:

> When the station of servitude is realized, then the divine light will shine upon the pure mirror of the heart.[36]

To understand how this process works it helps to recall that it is our spiritual nature that asks the inner questions as to what acts of service are appropriate in a given circumstance. In doing this, we reinforce for ourselves the reality that we are servants of God.

A ray of light from the universal divine mind (as described in chapter 8, 'Using the Faculty of Inner Vision') then illumines a relevant portion of the vast reservoir of knowledge available to our heart, so that it can be applied to the inner questions we have asked. This illuminating ray of knowledge becomes the basis for acts of service offered on behalf of our fellow servants of God, which moves all involved towards the presence of God, while also strengthening and defining our own unique identity and purpose.

When a genuine act of service emerges from the heart and enters the realm of action, the uniqueness of the individual also emerges.

Consequently, that light within our heart shines brighter, enabling us to see more of the reality and possibility contained there, and this makes possible increasingly complex acts of service. This upwardly and outwardly increasing 'building of the good', something that Jane Harper, author of *The Universe Within: A Guide to the Purpose of Life*, has called a 'virtuous cycle', is, like a spiral, without end or limit.

And lest we underestimate the power in the simplicity of such a wondrous process, we can recognize another beneficial outcome that she has described this way: 'As my virtuous powers developed, my physical, emotional, and intellectual powers became redirected and began to work together.'[37]

Indeed, our conscious willingness to move beyond mere imitation of the past to actively investigate reality helps to harmonize and coordinate all our powers and faculties towards their ultimate goal – working in unity to draw closer to that for which we have been created. This is the divine call for our inner reality in this age, just as it is the outer call for humanity as a whole.

We might say it is a call home to the sanctuary of the heart. The word 'sanctuary' has ancient and sacred origins and signifies a place of refuge, of absolute safety. Isn't that what we all yearn for, though most often, we seek it fruitlessly and frantically in the material world? We do this when we haven't yet truly recognized that it exists and already resides within us, and so we become the hunter, propelled by our lower nature.

Yet, even though we may lose contact with or forget the truth of our reality, or grow confused on the path, our lives can be continually graced with meeting those whose lives are immediate and beautiful reminders. We'll conclude with a story about one such soul, from Ron's early years:

I once knew an elderly woman of limited means named Erna Gutberlet. She lived on the outskirts of town and walked the three miles back and forth to her department store job every day without complaint. Like countless Bahá'ís all over the world, she contributed to the Fund, held Feast in her home and sought to offer Bahá'u'lláh's teachings to others while endeavouring to live in accordance with them herself.

One fall I painted her house and had a surprisingly good time. I have a vivid memory of resting on her sloping green lawn and seeing her slowly advance towards me with a pot of coffee and a pan of still-warm plum strudel. That was my pay and I considered myself well-paid indeed.

Sometimes, on leaving, I would ask her if she needed anything, in part, because my mother had told me to.

Her reply puzzled me for years. Erna said, 'I have everything I need. There are so many things I want but I have everything I need.'

I can still hear the peaceful tone of her voice and maybe that is why I have never forgotten her words.

Eventually I understood that she had found her way home. Not to the ramshackle old house that was falling apart around her but to the door of her own heart. She had walked through it and everything she needed was right there.

The Options Chart

Facet to be considered in determining an act of service	Optional	Not Optional	Chapter
Done out of love		X	10
Motivated out of an aspiration to selfless/universal love		X	10
Must be originated by spiritual nature		X	10
Actions result in greater humility		X	10
Actions must bring both parties closer to God		X	10

The whole, completed Options Chart can be found in appendix 1.

THE OPTIONS CHART: COMPLETED

As reference, we include here the two service questions.

1) At this moment in time, what is the act of service I am capable of giving that the other person is capable of receiving?

2) At this moment in time, what is the act of service I am capable of receiving that the other person is capable of giving?

Here is the completed Options Chart, a list of all of the facets to take into consideration when determining an act of service.

The Options Chart

Facet to be considered in determining an act of service	Optional	Not Optional	Chapter
Act must be generated by a servant of God		X	5
Act must be in conformity with the Covenant		X	5
Acts must come from the application of an attribute of God/virtue		X	6
Acts must be motivated by the pure love of God OR have a divine purpose OR have a human purpose linked with a divine purpose		X	6

Facet to be considered in determining an act of service	Optional	Not Optional	Chapter
We choose the specific purpose or virtue	X		6
Animated by the spirit of faith – person seeking scientific answer	X		7
Animated by the spirit of faith – person seeking spiritual answer		X	7
Must be guided by both the power of investigation and inner vision (requires listening, even to silence)		X	8
Must use our mind, animated by the spirit of faith, to make divinely principled choices that help bring us and others closer to God		X	9
Done out of love		X	10
Motivated out of an aspiration to selfless universal love		X	10
Must be originated by spiritual nature		X	10
Actions result in greater humility		X	10
Actions must bring both parties closer to God		X	10

SELECTED QUOTATIONS ABOUT OUR CREATED PURPOSES

I bear witness, O my God, that Thou hast created me to know Thee and to worship Thee.[1]

All praise and glory be to God Who, through the power of His might, hath delivered His creation from the nakedness of non-existence, and clothed it with the mantle of life. From among all created things He hath singled out for His special favour the pure, the gem-like reality of man, and invested it with a unique capacity of knowing Him and of reflecting the greatness of His glory. This twofold distinction conferred upon him hath cleansed away from his heart the rust of every vain desire, and made him worthy of the vesture with which his Creator hath deigned to clothe him. It hath served to rescue his soul from the wretchedness of ignorance.[2]

. . . Thou hast created me to remember Thee, to glorify Thee, and to aid Thy Cause.[3]

And when the sanctified souls rend asunder the veils of all earthly attachments and worldly conditions, and hasten to the stage of gazing on the beauty of the Divine Presence and are honoured by recognizing the Manifestation and are able to witness the splendour of God's Most Great Sign in their hearts, then will the purpose of creation, which is the knowledge of Him Who is the Eternal Truth, become manifest.[4]

The fruits of the tree of man have ever been and are goodly deeds and a praiseworthy character. Withhold not these fruits from the heedless. If they be accepted, your end is attained, and the purpose of life achieved.[5]

Thou wert created to bear and endure . . . [6]

Nevertheless, when faced with the irrevocable decree of the Almighty, the vesture that best befits us in this world is the vesture of patience and submission, and the most meritorious of all deeds is to commit our affairs into His hands and to surrender ourselves to His Will. Therefore, it behoves that leaf to take fast hold on the handle of resignation and radiant acquiescence and to strictly adhere to the cord of patience and long-suffering. God willing, through His aid and heavenly confirmation you may be enabled to exalt His Word and to render exemplary service to His Cause, that perchance the ears of all created things may be purged of the tales of bygone ages and become endued with the capacity to hearken to the holy verses that the Lord of all men has proclaimed. Indeed, this is the underlying purpose of man's existence during the brief period of his earthly life. Please God, we may all be confirmed and aided to achieve this.[7]

. . . Thou hast created Thy servants to aid Thy Cause and exalt Thy Word . . .[8]

All men have been created to carry forward an ever-advancing civilization.[9]

Ye were created to show love one to another and not perversity and rancour. Take pride not in love for yourselves but in love for your fellow-creatures.[10]

. . . all have been created to obey Him . . .[11]

To look after one's self only is therefore an animal propensity. It is the animal propensity to live solitary and alone. It is the animal proclivity to look after one's own comfort. But man was created to be a man – to be fair, to be just, to be merciful, to be kind to all his species, never to be willing that he himself be well off while others are in misery and distress – this is an attribute of the animal and not of man. Nay, rather, man should be willing to accept hardships for himself in order that others may enjoy wealth; he should enjoy trouble for himself that others may enjoy happiness and well-being. This is the attribute of man. This is becoming of man. Otherwise man is not man – he is less than the animal.

The man who thinks only of himself and is thoughtless of others is undoubtedly inferior to the animal because the animal is not possessed of the reasoning faculty. The animal is excused; but in man there is reason, the faculty of justice, the faculty of mercifulness. Possessing all these faculties he must not leave them unused. He who is so hard-hearted as to think only of his own comfort, such an one will not be called man.[12]

'What is the purpose of our lives?'
'Abdu'l-Bahá: 'To acquire virtues.'[13]

The All-loving God created man to radiate the Divine light and to illumine the world by his words, action and life. If he is without virtue he becomes no better than a mere animal, and an animal devoid of intelligence is a vile thing.[14]

God has created men to love each other; but instead, they kill each other with cruelty and bloodshed. God has created them that they may cooperate and mingle in accord; but instead, they ravage, plunder and destroy in the carnage of battle. God has created them to be the cause of mutual felicity and peace; but instead, discord, lamentation and anguish rise from the hearts of the innocent and afflicted.[15]

It is evident, then, that the intended and especial function of man is to rescue and redeem himself from the inherent defects of nature and become qualified with the ideal virtues of Divinity.[16]

All men must be treated equally. This is inherent in the very nature of humanity.[17]

The divine purpose is that men should live in unity, concord and agreement and should love one another. Consider the virtues of the human world and realize that the oneness of humanity is the primary foundation of them all.[18]

Ours rather is the duty to believe that the world-wide community of the Most Great Name . . . can . . . rise to the level of their calling and discharge their functions . . . Theirs is the duty to hold, aloft and undimmed, the torch of Divine guidance . . . Theirs is the function . . . to witness to the vision . . . of that re-created society, that Christ-promised Kingdom . . . [19]

The whole purpose of Bahá'u'lláh is that we should become a new kind of people, people who are upright, kind, intelligent, truthful, and honest and who live according to His great laws laid down for this new epoch in man's development. To call ourselves Bahá'ís is not enough, our inmost being must become ennobled and enlightened through living a Bahá'í life. [20]

REFERENCES FOR STATEMENTS ABOUT BLIND IMITATION

The following quotations are the source of the action statements in chapter 2.

- '. . . imitation of ancestral beliefs have hindered the progress of humanity thousands of years.'[1]

- Through imitation we 'find points of disagreement and division' among religions, the 'foundations' of which 'are one'.[2]

- One who holds to imitation 'is lacking in love for humanity' and 'manifests hatred and bigotry'.[3]

- Imitation produces 'enmity and strife', 'jealousy', 'war and bloodshed'.[4]

- Imitation prevents the refreshment provided by 'the downpouring of rain of mercy' and illumination 'by the rays of the Sun of Truth'.[5]

- 'Imitation destroys the foundation of religion . . .'[6]

- Imitation 'extinguishes the spirituality of the human world'.[7]

- Imitation 'deprives man of the knowledge of God'.[8]

- Imitation is 'the cause of the victory of materialism and infidelity over religion'.[9]

- Imitation is 'the denial of Divinity and the law of revelation'.[10]

- Imitation 'refuses Prophethood and rejects the Kingdom of God'.[11]

- 'So long as these imitations remain, the oneness of the world of humanity is impossible.'[12]

- Blind imitations 'have invariably become the cause of bitterness and hatred and have filled the world with darkness and violence of war'.[13]

- 'The greatest cause of bereavement and disheartening in the world of humanity is ignorance based upon blind imitation. It is due to this that wars and battles prevail; from this cause hatred and animosity arise continually among mankind.'[14]

- So long as imitation persists, 'strife and contention will destroy the purpose of religion and make love and fellowship impossible'.[15]

- '. . . the root cause of prejudice is blind imitation of the past – imitation in religion, in racial attitudes, in national bias, in politics.'[16]

- Blind imitation 'stunts the mind'.[17]

- Imitation prevents focus on 'new principles', which are 'the light of this time and the very spirit of this age'.[18]

- As long as imitation persists, 'humanity will find neither happiness nor rest nor composure'.[19]

The following quotations support the points made in chapter 2.

- 'God has not intended man to imitate blindly his fathers and ancestors.'[20]

- '. . . mere imitation' is 'fruitless'.[21]

- '. . . imitations have ever been a cause of disappointment and misguidance' and keep subjects from being 'clear'.[22]

- Imitation has 'adulterated human belief'.[23]

- Imitation 'transforms heavenly illumination into darkness'.[24]

- Imitation removes 'the heavenly light of divine truth' and sits people 'in the darkness' of 'imaginations'.[25]

- Imitations are 'mere superstitions' causing people to 'deny religion'.[26]

- Imitation causes people to be 'bereft and deprived of the radiance of religion'.[27]

- Imitation has made it 'impossible for the followers of religion to meet together in fellowship and agreement'; 'contact and communication have been considered contaminating', with the outcome of 'complete alienation and mutual bigotry'.[28]

- Imitation is 'the source of darkness in the world'.[29]

- Imitation has caused 'hatred and hostility' to appear in the world rather than 'unity and love'.[30]

- Imitation is the 'cause of disunion and dismemberment'.[31]

- As long as imitations are followed, 'animosity and discord will exist and increase'.[32]

- 'So long as they adhere to various imitations and are deprived of reality, strife and warfare will continue and rancour and sedition prevail.'[33]

- Imitation has caused 'wars and battles', 'division, discord and hatred'.[34]

- Imitation exposes humanity to 'direst peril'.[35]

- Imitation is the 'central and fundamental source of animosity among men, the obstacle of human progress, the cause of warfare and strife, the destroyer of peace, composure and welfare in the world'.[36]

- Imitations are the 'destroyers of human foundations established by the heavenly Educators'.[37]

- Imitation binds 'the world of humanity in the chains and fetters of ignorance'.[38]

- '. . . senseless imitation . . . is the principal reason why men fall away into paths of ignorance and degradation.' [39]

- 'Inasmuch as imitations differ, enmity and dissension have resulted.'[40]

- 'When imitations appeared, sects and denominations were formed' in Christianity.[41]

- 'The dogmas and blind imitations which gradually obscured the reality of the religion of God proved to be Israel's destructive influences, causing the expulsion of these chosen people from the Holy Land of their Covenant and promise.'[42]

- 'It is also essential to abstain from hypocrisy and blind imitation, inasmuch as their foul odour is soon detected by every man of understanding and wisdom.'[43]

APPENDIX 4

THE GUIDANCE OF SOULS

It is better to guide one soul than to possess all that is on earth, for as long as that guided soul is under the shadow of the Tree of Divine Unity, he and the one who hath guided him will both be recipients of God's tender mercy . . .[1]

It is interesting to note that in the above passage, the Báb repeats the word 'guide' as He describes the power and effects of this very significant service.

Among the variations of meaning that dictionaries offer for 'guide', two that occur repeatedly and are worth reflecting on are 'show' and 'point to'. Or, put another way, to draw attention to or towards, perhaps.

Such an act, different definitions suggest, implies an ability to recognize and keep to the way oneself, which may be unknown or unmapped for others, and the possession of intimate, experience-based knowledge of its potential or unexpected challenges, as well as its potential gifts.

In contemplating this particular act of unfolding service, let's revisit the two service questions and also the key guiding paragraph from the 1974 letter of Universal House of Justice on material suffering:

1) At this moment in time, what is the act of service I am capable of giving that the other person is capable of receiving?

2) At this moment in time, what is the act of service I am capable of receiving that the other person is capable of giving?

It is not merely material well-being that people need. What they desperately need is to know how to live their lives – **they need to know who they are, to what purpose they exist, and how**

they should act towards one another; and, once they know the answers to these questions they **need to be helped to gradually apply these answers to everyday behaviour.**[2]

Bahá'u'lláh's Revelation has invited each and every soul to investigate his or her reality and released the forces required to do so. Each of us now stands at the shore of an ocean from which we are invited to 'take our portion' – to discover and draw upon our uniquely created identity and our uniquely individual purpose.

To the degree that we truly investigate our own spiritual reality, to that same degree will we be true and effective servants, each in our very own way. If our knowledge of who we are and what our purpose is becomes the basis for our acts of service, we will not only draw closer to the source that has created us in and out of love but will embody and extend that love, which welcomes others to draw nearer to what is of God, too.

The Role of Identity in the Guidance of Souls

If our true identity is that of a servant of God, then logically the only reality-based acts we can perform are acts of service. Actions generated by any other perceived identity or purpose cause us to drift off the path of service into an illusory condition, one that inevitably brings suffering.

Let's consider again that the name 'servant of God' has no real meaning outside the all-encompassing context of God's Covenant. This concept can be represented by concentric circles in which the outermost circle, 'C', is the Covenant and 'S', the next inner circle, represents the Servant of God.

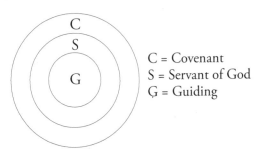

C = Covenant
S = Servant of God
G = Guiding

Our true identity, that of a servant of God, is contained within this Covenant. The 'G' in the innermost circle represents the act of service implied in seeking to offer guidance as we grow together with other souls on a path of investigation and learning.

When we seek to assist others through this, that previously quoted passage from the Báb tells us, both souls will 'be recipients of God's tender mercy' as long we are 'under the shadow of the Tree of Divine Unity' – operating within the shelter and embrace of the Covenant.

Hence in the diagram above, the act of service, guiding, is encompassed by the true identity of all souls, servant of God, which is contained within that Covenant.

In order to understand the concept of offering the service of guidance to another soul, we need to perceive this prospect in the context of who we really are – a servant of God – and the 'world' we truly live in – the Covenant of God.

The following passage from 'Abdu'l-Bahá suggests that seeking to offer guidance for other souls is an act of service – either giving or receiving – that can invite souls around us towards the presence of God.

> Under all conditions, the teaching must be carried forward, but with wisdom . . . and thus engender spirituality and fellowship among the children of men. If, for example, each and every one of the believers would become a true friend . . . conducting himself with absolute rectitude, associate with this soul, treat him with the utmost kindness, himself exemplify the divine instructions he hath received, the good qualities and behaviour patterns, and at all times act in accordance with the admonitions of God – it is certain that little by little he will succeed in awakening that previously heedless individual, and in changing his ignorance to knowledge of the truth.[3]

Here 'Abdu'l-Bahá has provided the true context for this vital act of service. We are exhorted to act with 'wisdom' and 'thus engender spirituality and fellowship'. Souls are to be treated with 'the utmost kindness' as we 'become a true friend' and, with love and 'absolute rectitude' (integrity), 'exemplify the divine instructions'.

In other words, we are invited to act from our spiritual nature, that aspect of our reality in which we are most closely connected with our divine source and with other souls. Such an act of service is, inherently, going to catalyse our own growth, as well as encourage that of others. As we recognize and manifest such qualities of our soul as wisdom, kindness and love, we come into contact with those very resources that are essential in every area of life in which we seek relationship.

This is a very significant reality that can also free us from any number of illusions that may hold us hostage and cause us suffering. While the world appears to demand different 'faces' or multiple identities of us, we are invited, instead, to turn towards and embrace what is real, at the essence of our own heart, the dwelling place of true unity, with ourselves, with others and with God. What bounty is there greater than this?

As 'Abdu'l-Bahá has described:

> Let all be set free from the multiple identities that were born of passion and desire, and in the oneness of their love for God, find a new way of life.[4]

Indeed, when we yearn for the building of the good, in every life, we serve both others' needs and our own. We find and perceive the self in the other and see the 'other' as our very self.

The Role of Purpose in the Guidance of Souls

The following allegory, 'Stone-cutters' Village', illustrates what life is like when souls have mastered the art of placing acts of service in context.

A long time ago, there was a village famous for the work of its stone-cutters. As its children walked to school or to play, there were tables placed along the pathways and roadways. From the earliest age the children were taught to stop at these tables, each of which held a hammer, a chisel and some rocks. The children were encouraged to experiment with picking up the chisel, holding it absolutely straight and striking the rock. They were also gradually taught that they needed to concentrate on how they held the chisel and where it was placed on the rock and then focus on striking the chisel head firmly with the hammer.

Time went by and eventually all the rocks were evenly split on all the tables. No one felt as though he or she was solely responsible for splitting the rocks, although everyone had experienced hitting a rock and having it split open. Each knew that his or her blow, which had produced the visible result of splitting the rock, was merely one of dozens of hammer blows.

The children grew up to take their place as skilled stone-cutters but, more importantly, they grew up with humility as they approached their work and an appreciation for the united effort that produced it.

Because the overall focus was on the process instead of the outcome, the village prospered. In fact, the process created a sense of community among the villagers and the overall purpose became maintaining that sense of community and, thus, continuing to prosper.

Within that process, every person in the village felt responsibility for the training of the next generation of stone-cutters. The challenge facing the villagers was how well they could connect **purpose, process and event** (the striking of the stones with the hammer and chisel), because true meaning emerges when those connections are properly made. And for human souls, where there is meaning, there is growth and life.

We can keep in mind this story, with its message about the importance of concentrating on the individual steps in a process, as we consider this next experiment. It has three elements, the same three elements featured in the story: purpose, process and event.

The first step is to visualize someone who you have seen is attracted to investigating reality and advancing closer to God. Obviously this is a possibility for every soul but, in our lives, certain encounters reflect this to us in more evident ways, ones that our heart is well-equipped to perceive.

As a part of this process it will be necessary to seek the assistance of inner vision, which we can best access through silence ('Close one eye and open the other'⁵) and through prayer, meditation and reflection – i.e. *listening* with our inner ear.

One good time to do this is just prior to sleep, when you can also ask what act of service you might offer such a soul, what might bring both of you closer to God, and pray that both you and this soul will be guided towards what divine direction knows is part of a building of the good.

Now we ask that you draw an unusual ladder.

Based on the inspiration that comes to your heart, write on the bottom rung of the ladder what your beginning act of service will be. As we have said, this is a very unusual ladder. It has a bottom rung but no top rung because the journey towards what is of God is infinite.

However, we do also need some tangible goal, so arbitrarily label a higher rung somewhere on the ladder 'Recognize as soul', a recognition that you will somehow seek to offer directly, perhaps by acknowledging and verbalizing the goodness you perceive in that person or in his or her actions. You may even choose to make this your initial act of service. If this seems unusual, then reflect on how rarely in day-to-day life souls receive this kind of reflection or acknowledgement.

On an even higher rung, you might add 'Visit to offer accompaniment or support as a soul' or 'Extend hospitality and love'. Succeeding rungs could include 'Share a spiritual conversation', 'Offer relevant reflection from sacred guidance' or 'Share prayer and devotional time together'. The rungs can just keep going on with no end.

In this experiment, the **event** is an act of service. Earlier in the book we made a statement that the condition of servitude is the most powerful and efficient means for the transference of energy in all the worlds of God. Bahá'u'lláh, in the *Epistle to the Son of the Wolf*, says: 'The Imam Ṣádiq hath said: "Servitude is a substance, the essence of which is Divinity."'[6]

The second step is to ask that divine assistance will increase your capacity for offering even purer and more selfless acts of service. And that the capacity of the recipient of your act of service will, likewise, be increased.

What you are doing in this process is continually rechannelling the divine assistance that is needed for forward movement and momentum. Only our lack of faith in the power of divine assistance, or our ego-based belief that we are the source of this transformative power, can hinder or thwart this process. The process itself is comprised of willing and heartfelt cumulative acts of service, with the overall purpose that both souls advance continually towards the presence of God.

While the process is necessarily a mysterious one, as it involves one mysterious creation of God seeking to serve another, the very practical approach of being systematic and having goals will help to focus energy in the most beneficial direction.

We are in a learning mode. No one has ever built the Kingdom of God on earth before, yet in this age, this is what we have been invited to do. It is sacred work and it requires the most sacred aspect of that great mystery of ourselves. Everything we are doing is new, and to be truly new, it must be non-ego-willed (N-E-W) and requires our full and best attention. The promised outcome is indescribably joyous and glorious. It is worth our paying attention and learning from this grandest of experiments in the story of humankind.

In the stone-cutters' village, the children were taught to strike the stone to the utmost of their capacity. They took no credit if they were the one whose hammer blow happened to split the stone. They realized they were one part of a much larger process and they were content, and also thankful, to play that part.

So it is for servants of God focusing to the utmost of our capacity on the greatest possible expression of our true identity and purpose: acts of service.

THE GUIDING LIGHT OF THE FEAR OF GOD

This is not an exhaustive study of all the connotations of the fear of God or of fear in general. What we wish to explore here is a connection between what is offered in the chapter on purpose and the possibility of eliminating some harmful aspects of fear in our lives while keeping the beneficial behavioural restraints of the fear of God.

Bahá'ís do not believe in the God of annihilation, and lack of faith in immortality is understood to be a cause of fear and weakened power:

> The conception of annihilation is a factor in human degradation, a cause of human debasement and lowliness, a source of human fear and abjection.[1]

We need to hold in our hearts a sense of breathtaking awe and reverence about the life with which we are entrusted and the fear of damaging our relationship with God. We also need to understand the ways in which we can damage this sacred relationship because there is a direct connection between increasing the healthy fear of God and decreasing unhealthy fears.

> And if he feareth not God, God will make him to fear all things . . .[2]

The gist of this exercise is that, if we understand the inner signals of fear generated by the soul, the purpose of which is educational, we can then quickly make the needed corrections in behaviour that will prevent us from developing an unhealthy and painful mental state of being that is consumed by fear. This debilitating mental state has been described by the theologian Paul Tillich as existential anxiety or spiritual anxiety.

It is often easier to understand an intangible spiritual concept by focusing on its tangible physical counterpart. One concept that explains the relationship between the spiritual and material world is indispensable to learning how to dispel fear and anxiety.

> 'The Celestial Universe is so formed that the under world reflects the upper world.' That is to say whatever exists in heaven is reflected in this phenomenal world.[3]

> . . . the outward is the expression of the inward; the earth is the mirror of the Kingdom; the material world corresponds to the spiritual world.[4]

The spiritual world reflects the material world and the material world reflects the spiritual world.

We can understand the concept of living in a spiritual world of firm parameters because we live with physical laws such as gravity every day. Indeed, the underlying purpose of the material world could be to smooth our transition to a purely spiritual world – a world which we know to be our future home.

Here's an experiment to try: Close your eyes and imagine you are walking on the sidewalk, lost in your own thoughts, in the heart of a very busy town. As you approach a curb, you are surprised by the very loud sound of a truck horn. This frightening sound occurs just as you are ready to step onto the street.

Without thinking, you instantly pull your foot back to the sidewalk. Your heart is pounding and you are shivering with fear. The fear subsides when you look up to see the truck moving away from you in the distance. The reason the fear subsides so quickly is that the fear was clearly **identifiable**. The mind had pictured a truck fast approaching and then realized just as quickly that the threat had passed. But there are also **unidentifiable fears** whose origin we don't fully understand. These unidentifiable fears create anxieties that tend to become more long lasting because the root cause is so difficult to discern – hence they become an unseen, untreated wound that worsens over time. We will explain more about this subject in the coming pages.

For the purposes of this exercise we are defining fear as an identifiable threat and anxiety as an unidentifiable threat.

Let's return to our example of the truck horn and the pedestrian. What has occurred is that your physical survival mechanism (see chapter 10 on the spiritual nature) sent you a fear signal that your physical self was in danger. The signal was received and you took action, so the fear signal was educational and a form of guidance.

A serious problem arises when the purpose of the fear signal is a mystery because its source is the unseen spiritual world that our reality, the soul, inhabits. If we are alone in a pitch-black room where unknown threats to our survival come at us from all sides, our fear simply intensifies with the passage of time. What is needed is for the light of perception to shine so that we can see the door that allows us to leave this room. This is the purpose of this exercise.

Referring back to the quotation that confirms that the outward is a reflection of the inward, the all-important question becomes:

What is the spiritual equivalent of our physical self or identity and what is the spiritual equivalent of our physical survival mechanism?

The Bahá'í writings describe three identities or conditions of existence:

> Know that the conditions of existence are limited to the conditions of servitude, of prophethood and of Deity . . .[5]

The model that Bahá'u'lláh offered to humanity for how to live our lives is 'Abdu'l-Bahá. He eschewed all titles except that of 'Servant of God'. It follows that we too are servants of God, and from other writings we know that we are immortal souls that have a beginning but not an end. **Therefore we can say that the spiritual equivalent of our physical self or identity is an immortal servant of God.**

In the experiment of the truck horn above, we observed that at the first sign of a threat to our physical self, a fear signal, which has been refined through the ages by evolution, directed our behaviour.

In the spiritual world, at the first sign of a threat to our spiritual identity as an immortal servant of God, a signal that we will call 'the fear of (losing our connection to) God signal' has been refined through the ages by successive divine revelations. This occurs within our spiritual nature, for which, we suggest, the spiritual equivalent of physical evolution is the Covenant of God.

Here are some quotations that describe how the fear of God is designed to be a form of educational guidance:

> And if, confirmed by the Creator, the lover escapes from the claws of the eagle of love, he will enter the Valley of Knowledge and come out of doubt into certitude, and turn from the darkest of illusion to the **guiding light of the fear of God**. His inner eyes will open and he will privily converse with his Beloved; he will set ajar the gate of truth and piety, and shut the doors of vain imaginings.[6]

Notice the quotation says the 'guiding light of the fear of God'. If we return to the image of standing alone in a dark room and not knowing where the threats are coming from, we can imagine being consumed by fear when, suddenly, the lights go on. Our fear doesn't go away instantaneously but the origin of the threats can now be identified. We can now move from the far worse state of anxiety, which is defined as an **unidentifiable threat**, to a state of fear, which is defined as an **identifiable threat**. The addition of light into a pitch-black room where we might have felt like a trapped animal has shown us an exit door out of this terrible mental state. For some, it is the first step out of hell.

The fear of God has ever been the prime factor in the education of His creatures. Well is it with them that have attained thereunto![7]

The Solution

If we reflect on that original example of stepping back onto the curb when a truck horn sounded, we see that it was a fear signal, a potentially life-saving signal, that prompted us to move quickly. In effect, we were guided and educated by the fear signal generated by our survival mechanism.

What, then, might trigger a corresponding spiritual threat to our true identity, which would then activate the signal of our fear of losing our connection to God?

This signal is triggered when we cross the line of moderation and form an attachment to some aspect of the material world. Say, for example, that we are spending far too much time on a hobby such as playing golf or collecting butterflies, to the extent that we are neglecting our responsibilities or our loved ones.

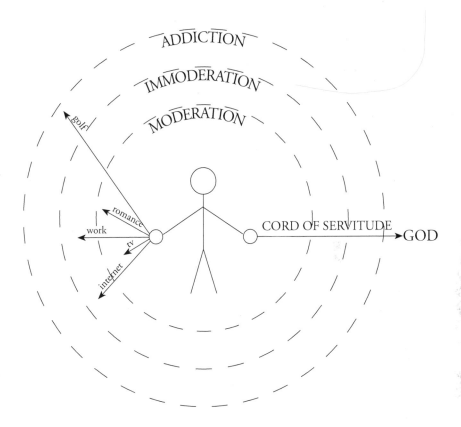

The true self, the immortal servant of God, becomes confused and fearful and begins asking questions: 'If I am an immortal being, why am I so attached to golf or butterflies – why am I so attached to mortality? If I am a servant of God, why am I now serving a golf ball or a dead butterfly? I feel lost, confused and fearful and the "cord of servitude" that connects me to God is becoming frayed and in danger of being severed.'

> Cling, O ye people of Bahá, to the **cord of servitude** unto God, the True One, **for thereby your stations shall be made manifest**, your names written and preserved, your ranks raised and your memory exalted in the Preserved Tablet. **Beware lest the dwellers on earth hinder you from this glorious and exalted station.**[8]

Notice the link between 'your stations', your identity as a servant of God and clinging to the 'cord of servitude'. The threat to our identity comes from the **dwellers on earth** – a threat that exists in the material world. When we cross the bounds of moderation we begin to let go of the cord of servitude to God and we begin clinging to aspects of the material world. When we are attached to that world we are detached from the spiritual world.

The rule of thumb is that for every attachment we make, we gain an unhealthy fear and we can easily become overwhelmed by unhealthy fears. The choice is to act on 'the fear of (losing our connection to) God signal' and detach ourselves from material things or eventually become **possessed** by fear and suffering. There are dire physical, mental and spiritual consequences if this signal is not understood.

And if he feareth not God, God will make him to fear all things . . .⁹

Easy to say, but how does one actually sever an attachment to the material world? First, let us examine how the Bahá'í writings define detachment. In the following quotation 'Abdu'l-Bahá explains the concepts of detachment and attachment:

Detachment does not consist in setting fire to one's house, or becoming bankrupt or throwing one's fortune out of the window, or even giving away all of one's possessions. **Detachment consists in refraining from letting our possessions possess us.** A prosperous merchant who is not absorbed in his business knows severance. A banker whose occupation does not prevent him from serving humanity is severed. A poor man can be attached to a small thing . . .

God has given man a heart and **the heart must have some attachment**. We have proved that nothing is completely worthy of our heart's devotion save reality, for all else is destined to perish. Therefore the heart is never at rest and never finds real joy and happiness until it attaches itself to the eternal. How foolish the bird that builds its nest in a tree that may perish when it could build its nest in an ever-verdant garden of paradise.¹⁰

What an incredibly clear definition: 'Detachment consists in refraining from letting our possessions possess us.'

Man must attach himself to an infinite reality, so that his glory, his joy, and his progress may be infinite. Only the spirit is real; everything else is as shadow. All bodies are disintegrated in the end; only reality subsists.[11]

'Abdu'l-Bahá's definition of reality is what does not 'perish' or die. He is telling us in the above quotation that we should not be attached to what will come to an end. We are, in effect, attaching ourselves to death, which confuses and frightens our immortal soul, and the more we make this mistake, the more we will be full of anxiety.

'The heart must have some attachment.' The heart will serve some entity and our identity will be defined by that primary attachment.

Our heart will attach to something. It does not have a choice because we are dependent beings or 'contingent beings'.[12]

It is necessary to act on 'the fear of (losing our connection to) God' signal quickly, so that fear educates and guides us instead of hurting us. The other reason that we want to react quickly to that signal is that the quicker we react, the quicker the fear signal will subside.

Love is a light that never dwelleth in a heart possessed by fear.[13]

The word 'dwelleth' is significant in that it implies a time frame. A child touching a hot stove is only harmed if the finger is not quickly removed. If removed right away, the pain, which causes fear, is educational.

The choice is ours. We can live in a house of love that God has built for us or we can live in a house of fear that we have built for ourselves.

The fear signal, if not addressed, ceases to become educational and becomes extremely harmful. **Eventually our identity becomes that of a servant of fear rather than a servant of God.**

We want to learn to recognize the signals and react quickly because the fear will only intensify. When we were children and put our hand on a stove and then removed the hand immediately, we had a physically harmless educational experience. If we had left our hand on the stove for a prolonged period of time, we would have experienced increasing amounts of pain and fear.

So how do we escape the clutches of attachment and fear? How do we detach ourselves from what is harmful and attach ourselves to what is beneficial?

The first step is to reinforce our true identity.

Cling, O ye people of Bahá, to the cord of servitude unto God, the True One, for thereby your stations shall be made manifest, your names written and preserved, your ranks raised and your memory exalted in the Preserved Tablet.[14]

'Abdu'l-Bahá eschewed all titles bestowed upon Him by Bahá'u'lláh except one: 'Servant of God'. The same follows for each of us, as immortal mysteries of God:

I, _____, am an immortal servant of God. I was born an immortal servant of God. I was not born to serve objects or ideologies. I will live eternally as an immortal servant of God.

I, _____, am not a writer, a plumber, a high school student, a husband, a wife – and I am most definitely not a servant of my golf game.

I, _____, am an immortal servant of God who writes books, fixes broken pipes, goes to school, is married and plays golf for moderate recreation.

I, _____, will never find my unique identity and will live a life consumed by unhealthy fear unless I first and foremost have it clear in my mind that I am a servant of God.

The 'cord of servitude' must be attached to God and not to any material object or activity.

One experience of Ron's illustrated for him the connection between identity and fear: In her last year of college, his oldest daughter, a gifted writer, often procrastinated about getting writing assignments done on time. One night when she was due to hand in a poem the next morning and hadn't yet done the work, she was filled with fear and anxiety. As she and Ron talked about the source of her feelings, Ron reminded her that she was not a writer or a poet. She was an immortal servant of God who wrote poetry.

He told her, 'When you think you are a poet, you have linked an illusory identity with the poem that is due the next day and have thus linked the success of that poem with your survival. Suddenly you are back in a predator-filled jungle aeons ago and your primitive emotional brain is activating the survival mechanism with its concomitant fear signals.'

She began to relax and even to laugh. After that she was able to interpret the fear signals more quickly in her life and consequently leave a world of illusion much sooner by centring herself on her true identity as a servant of God.

It is vital that we do not confuse what we do with who we are. If we make this mistake our soul sends to our immediate consciousness a fear signal that our true identity is being compromised.

The goal of this exercise is to break the unhealthy attachments that create unhealthy fears, and the key to that process is the concept of purpose alluded to in this quotation:

> O thou son of the Kingdom! All things are beneficial if **joined** with the love of God; and without His love, all things are harmful, and act as a veil between man and the Lord of the Kingdom. When His love is there, every bitterness turneth sweet, and every bounty rendereth a wholesome pleasure.[15]

Any act that we perform without the love of God as a motivating purpose creates 'a veil between man and the Lord of the Kingdom' and results in a state of indentured servitude to all things fleeting and material.

This means that if we take Mrs Smith to the Feast and have no love in our heart, Mrs Smith will arrive at the Feast but the veil that we have created will make it more difficult to find our way to our intended spiritual destination.

It helps to make a list of the recurring activities that occupy your day such as work, hobbies, eating, interacting with friends and family, etc. The telltale sign that we have formed an unhealthy attachment is when we or the people around us notice an imbalance. For example: Could we be working far longer than it is really necessary? Are we eating or drinking way too much? Are we playing a sport too often or watching too much television? And when we are not excessively engaged in these activities, are we excessively thinking about them?

Another telltale sign is not being honest with ourselves and others about how much time we engage in thinking about and undertaking certain material pursuits. Self-delusion makes it even more difficult to find our way out of the internal maze such imbalances create.

The state of imbalance is a sign that we have formed an unhealthy attachment of some kind. Our heart may be serving our occupation or whatever substances we feel compelled to consume, thus distorting our identity. Our new identity could become 'servant of the golf club' or 'servant of the club sandwich'.

The Solution: Merge a Spiritual Purpose with a Material Activity

The all-important step in severing this unhealthy attachment is to join a material activity with a spiritual purpose – one consistent with being an immortal servant of God. If we can come up with a spiritual purpose for playing golf or collecting butterflies, then the fear signal will vanish, along with the 'veil between man and the Lord of the Kingdom'.

By doing this we will be able to enjoy whatever we do on a material and spiritual level without forming a dangerous attachment. The other great benefit in this merger is that an act of service with a spiritual purpose brings eternal results, both for the development of our soul and the effects it can create. One loving act can enrich the world in unseen and unimaginable ways.

Our inability to join a spiritual purpose consistent with the Covenant of Bahá'u'lláh to a material activity is a warning sign that either the material activity is not healthy or that the activity has become excessive.

But when we join and relate these two kinds of purposes, we can achieve a middle way, a balance, whereby we avoid the extremes of getting caught in the material world's frenzy on the one hand and isolating ourselves as if cloistered on the other.

The final step is that the spiritual purpose must generate an act of service that benefits us and others, and by 'benefit' we mean 'bring us closer to God'. Without this action step no change will occur.

We reinforce our identity as a servant of God when we engage in acts of service.

Let's revisit the two service questions and remember that the daily use of these will create a balance not only between our ability to give and receive but between all our inner and outer powers and faculties. Remember, these are inner questions that we ask ourselves.

1) At this moment in time, what is the act of service I am capable of giving that the other person is capable of receiving?

2) At this moment in time, what is the act of service I am capable of receiving that the other person is capable of giving?

The Role of the Spiritual Nature in Merging Material and Spiritual Purposes

Here is an exercise that we can do by ourselves or in a classroom setting:

Connect a fear with some facet of your life. Let's use money issues as an example. Chapter 10, 'Coming Home to Our Spiritual Nature', explains the three natures of the human being and how they relate to one another. Each nature has a different level of perception, which in turn creates a different set of needs.

Animal Nature: The animal nature is concerned with survival right now, in this moment. Is there money for food and shelter right now? Is there money for other physical needs right now?

Human Nature: The human nature is concerned with survival today **and** tomorrow. Is there money for food and shelter for the present and the future? Is there money for other material needs such as intellectual pursuits, hobbies, recreation, etc.?

Spiritual Nature: The spiritual nature has exactly the same concerns about the need for adequate money for survival. But the higher nature has a more expansive definition of survival.

In fact, each of the three natures defines survival based on its conception of how it perceives its identity. The spiritual nature is concerned with having adequate money to fulfil the kinds of actions that it knows will have an enduring effectiveness that goes far beyond our individual lives. The task of the spiritual nature is to recognize, balance and then merge the legitimate purposes of all three natures into one common purpose.

The all-important final step is to translate the merged material and spiritual purposes into acts of service that are in harmony with the Covenant of Bahá'u'lláh. In chapter 4, 'The Two Service Questions', we said that long-term use of these inner questions would lead to a balance between all our powers and faculties. These questions also contribute to achieving a harmonious balance between our three natures. The parameters of the structure of the Covenant of Bahá'u'lláh prevent the individual from straying beyond the bounds of moderation. This safeguard also results in the severing of unhealthy attachments or, better yet, not forming unhealthy attachments in the first place.

A word of warning. The ultimate destination of an unhealthy attachment is addiction.

The wonderful result of freeing ourselves from unhealthy attachments is that we also eliminate the unhealthy fears that dampen our inner spiritual senses. Each time we eliminate an unhealthy attachment, we also eliminate the fear associated with that attachment. Finally, all that is left is the guiding light of the fear of God signal, and this 'guiding light' leads to the most wonderful outcome of all:

His inner eyes will open and he will privily converse with his Beloved . . .[16]

Notice the word 'converse' with its connotation of a two-way interchange – a wonderful prospect indeed!

Releasing ourselves from unhealthy attachments and the accompanying fears makes it possible for us to 'privily converse' with all the loved ones in our lives, in this world and the next.

Here is an exercise that demonstrates the possibilities in this last statement.

Choose five people. Then secretly ask one of them to say or sing a short prayer no matter what the group is told to do. Announce to the five that at the count of three they should all talk loudly about what causes them fear.

It might also be helpful to ask the person saying or singing the prayer to recite or read this quotation:

When the channel of the human soul is cleansed of all worldly and impeding attachments, it will unfailingly perceive the breath of the Beloved across immeasurable distances, and will, led by its perfume, attain and enter the City of Certitude.[17]

After a time, tap each person in the group on the shoulder and tell him or her to stop talking, leaving only the person who is saying the quotation still speaking. The tapping on the shoulder is symbolic of getting rid of an attachment and the fear that comes with that attachment. The only fear left is the guiding light of the fear of God.

Let's delve into this subject a little more deeply. We all have someone in our life that we truly love a lot – a husband, a wife, a son, a daughter or a best friend. Imagine right now that there might be a **possibility** that you would never be in this person's presence again in all the worlds of God. There would be many emotions connected with that dreadful possibility. Surely one such emotion would be fear. But the fear would only exist because you experienced love in that person's presence at one time.

Keep this in mind as you read this Hidden Word:

O Son of Man! Veiled in My immemorial being and in the ancient eternity of My essence, I knew My love for thee; therefore I created thee, have engraved on thee Mine image and revealed to thee My beauty.[18]

We were created because God loves us. He loved us and then created us. At one time we were a thought of God that took form to begin an eternal journey back to the awareness of God. The remembrance of the beauty of God is with us and we long to be reunited with Him. This is why the fear signal is generated when there is a threat of even temporarily delaying this homeward journey by forming an attachment in the material world.

The reason the fear of (losing our connection to) God signal is so unrelentingly powerful is that at the core of our being we have memories far beyond what our minds could ever imagine.

O My Friends! Have ye forgotten that true and radiant morn, when in those hallowed and blessed surroundings ye were all gathered in My presence beneath the shade of the tree of life, which is planted in the all-glorious paradise? Awe-struck ye listened as I gave utterance to these three most holy words: O friends! Prefer not your will to Mine, never desire that which I have not desired for you, and approach Me not with lifeless hearts, defiled with worldly desires and cravings. Would ye but sanctify your souls, ye would at this present hour recall that place and those surroundings, and the truth of My utterance should be made evident unto all of you.[19]

How much do we want to remember 'that true and radiant morn'?

BIBLIOGRAPHY

'Abdu'l-Bahá in London. London: Bahá'í Publishing Trust, 1982.

'Abdu'l-Bahá. *Foundations of World Unity*. Wilmette, IL: Bahá'í Publishing Trust, 1979.

— *Paris Talks*. London: Bahá'í Publishing Trust, 1995.

— *The Promulgation of Universal Peace*. Wilmette, IL: Bahá'í Publishing Trust, 1982.

— *The Secret of Divine Civilization*. Wilmette, IL: Bahá'í Publishing Trust, 1990.

— *Selections from the Writings of 'Abdu'l-Bahá*. Haifa: Bahá'í World Centre, 1978.

— *Some Answered Questions*. Wilmette, IL: Bahá'í Publishing Trust, 1981.

— *Tablets of the Divine Plan*. Wilmette, IL: Bahá'í Publishing Trust, 1993.

— *A Traveler's Narrative*. Wilmette, IL: Bahá'í Publishing Trust, 1980.

— *The Will and Testament of 'Abdu'l-Bahá*. Wilmette, IL: Bahá'í Publishing Trust, 1991.

The Báb. *Selections from the Writings of the Báb*. Haifa: Bahá'í World Centre, 1976.

Bahá'í International Community. *A Bahá'í Perspective on Drug Abuse Prevention* by A. M. Ghadirian. Published in *Bulletin on Narcotics*, vol. XLIII, no. 1, January 1991. BIC Document no. 91-0115. http://statements.bahai.org/91-0115.htm.

— *The Prosperity of Humankind*. New York: Bahá'í International Community United Nations Office, 1995.

Bahá'í Prayers: A Selection of Prayers revealed by Bahá'u'lláh, the Báb and 'Abdu'l-Bahá. Wilmette, IL: Bahá'í Publishing Trust, 2002.

Bahai Scriptures. New York: Brentano's, 1923.

The Bahá'í World. vols. 1–12, 1925–54. rpt. Wilmette, IL: Bahá'í Publishing Trust, 1980.

Bahá'í World Faith. Wilmette, IL: Bahá'í Publishing Trust, 1976.

Bahá'u'lláh. *Epistle to the Son of the Wolf*. Wilmette, IL: Bahá'í Publishing Trust, 1988.

— *Gems of Divine Mysteries: Javáhiru'l-Asrár.* Haifa: Bahá'í World Centre, 2002.

— *Gleanings from the Writings of Bahá'u'lláh.* Wilmette, IL: Bahá'í Publishing Trust, 1983.

— *The Hidden Words.* Wilmette, IL: Bahá'í Publishing Trust, 1990.

— *The Kitáb-i-Aqdas.* Haifa: Bahá'í World Centre, 1992.

— *Kitáb-i-Íqán.* Wilmette, IL: Bahá'í Publishing Trust, 1989.

— *Prayers and Meditations.* Wilmette, IL: Bahá'í Publishing Trust, 1987.

— *The Proclamation of Bahá'u'lláh.* Haifa: Bahá'í World Centre, 1967.

— *The Seven Valleys and the Four Valleys.* Wilmette, IL: Bahá'í Publishing Trust, 1991.

— *The Summons of the Lord of Hosts: Tablets of Bahá'u'lláh.* Haifa: Bahá'í World Centre, 2002.

— *Tabernacle of Unity.* Haifa: Bahá'í World Centre, 2006.

— *Tablets of Bahá'u'lláh.* Wilmette, IL: Bahá'í Publishing Trust, 1988.

Bahíyyih Khánum: The Greatest Holy Leaf. Haifa: Bahá'í World Centre, 1982.

Balyuzi, H. M. *'Abdu'l-Bahá: The Centre of the Covenant.* Oxford: George Ronald, 2nd ed. with minor corr. 1987.

Childre, Doc. *Freeze Frame: One Minute Stress Management: A Scientifically Proven Technique for Clear Decision Making and Improved Health.* Boulder Creek, CA: Planetary Publications, 1998.

The Compilation of Compilations. Prepared by the Universal House of Justice 1963–1990. 2 vols. [Mona Vale NSW]: Bahá'í Publications Australia, 1991.

Edelstein, Michael R. *Three Minute Therapy: Change Your Thinking, Change Your Life.* Centennial, CO: Glenbridge Publishing, 1997.

Faizi, Gloria. *The Bahá'í Faith: An Introduction.* Wilmette, IL: Bahá'í Publishing Trust, rev. ed. 1972.

Fisher, Roger and Alan Sharp. *Getting It Done: How to Lead When You're Not in Charge.* New York: HarperBusiness, 1999.

Frankl, Viktor E. *Man's Search for Meaning.* New York: Washington Square Press, 1985.

Goleman, Daniel. *Emotional Intelligence.* New York: Bantam Books, 1996.

— *Social Intelligence: The New Science of Human Relationships.* New York: Bantam Dell, 2006.

Harper, Jane E. *The Universe Within Us: A Guide to the Purpose of Life.* Wilmette, IL: Bahá'í Publishing Trust, 2009.

Hatcher, John S. *Close Connections: The Bridge Between Spiritual and Physical Reality.* Wilmette, IL: Bahá'í Publishing, 2005.

— *The Purpose of Physical Reality*. Wilmette, IL: Bahá'í Publishing Trust, 1987.

Hatcher, William S. *Love, Power and Justice*. Wilmette, IL: Bahá'í Publishing Trust, 2002.

Heggie, James. *An Index of Quotations from the Bahá'í Sacred Writings*. Oxford: George Ronald, 1983.

Japan Will Turn Ablaze. Japan: Bahá'í Publishing Trust, 1974.

Jordan, Daniel C. *Becoming Your True Self: How the Bahá'í Faith Releases Human Potential*. Wilmette, IL: Bahá'í Publishing Trust, 1980.

— *Comprehensive Deepening Program: A Process for Personal Transformation*. Wilmette, IL: Bahá'í Publishing Trust, 1973.

— *How the Bahá'í Faith Releases Human Potential*. Wilmette, IL: National Bahá'í Schools Committee, 1971.

Kaufman, Barry Neil. *Giant Steps*. New York: Fawcett Crest, 1979.

— *Happiness is a Choice*. New York: Fawcett Columbine, 1991.

— *To Love Is to Be Happy With*. New York: Fawcett Crest, 1977.

Kolstoe, John E. *Consultation: A Universal Lamp of Guidance*. Oxford: George Ronald, 1985.

— *Developing Genius*. Oxford: George Ronald, 1995.

Kurzius, Brian. *Fire and Gold: Benefiting from Life's Tests*. Oxford: George Ronald, 1995.

LeDoux, Joseph. *The Emotional Brain: The Mysterious Underpinnings of Emotional Life*. New York: Simon & Schuster, 1996.

Lights of Guidance: A Bahá'í Reference File. Compiled by Helen Hornby. New Delhi: Bahá'í Publishing Trust, 5th ed. 1997.

Lippitt, Marian Crist. *Introduction to the Worlds of God and Classifications of the Whole (or Reality) of Existence: Basis for Developing the 'Science of Reality'*. Unpublished manuscript.

— *Successful Self Direction*. Unpublished manuscript.

Living the Life. London: Bahá'í Publishing Trust, 1984.

Maḥmúd-i-Zarqání. *Maḥmúd's Diary*. Oxford: George Ronald, 1998.

Maslow, A. H. *Religions, Values, and Peak-Experiences*. New York: Penguin Books, 1994.

McGraw, Patricia Romano. *It's Not Your Fault: How Healing Relationships Change Your Brain and Can Help You Overcome a Painful Past*. Wilmette, IL: Bahá'í Publishing Trust, 2004.

Nelson, Portia. 'Autobiography in Five Short Chapters'. Various editions.

— *There's a Hole in My Sidewalk: The Romance of Self-Discovery.* Hillsboro, OR: Beyond Words, 1993.

Nicholas Green Foundation. www.nicholasgreen.org (accessed 22 July 2013).

One Common Faith. Commissioned by and prepared under the supervision of the Universal House of Justice. Wilmette, IL: Bahá'í Publishing Trust, 2005.

Palmer, Helen, ed. *Inner Knowing: Consciousness, Creativity, Insight, Intuition.* New York: Jeremy P. Tarcher/Putnam, 1998.

Rowshan, Arthur. *Stress: An Owner's Manual: Positive Techniques for Taking Charge of Your Life.* Oxford: Oneworld, rev. ed. 1997.

Ruhi Institute. *Teaching the Cause*: Book 6. Riviera Beach, FL: Palabra, 1998.

Saiedi, Nader. *Gate of the Heart: Understanding the Writings of the Báb.* Waterloo, ON: Wilfrid Laurier University Press, 2008.

Shoghi Effendi. *The Advent of Divine Justice.* Wilmette, IL: Bahá'í Publishing Trust, 1990.

— *Bahá'í Administration.* Wilmette, IL: Bahá'í Publishing Trust, 1995.

— *High Endeavors: Messages to Alaska.* [Anchorage]: National Spiritual Assembly of the Bahá'ís of Alaska, 1976.

— *Messages to America.* Wilmette, IL: Bahá'í Publishing Committee, 1947.

— *The World Order of Bahá'u'lláh.* Wilmette, IL: Bahá'í Publishing Trust, 1991.

Star of the West. rpt. Oxford: George Ronald, 1984.

Taherzadeh, Adib. *The Child of the Covenant.* Oxford, George Ronald, 2000.

— *The Covenant of Bahá'u'lláh.* Oxford: George Ronald, 1992.

— *The Revelation of Bahá'u'lláh*, vol. 1. Oxford: George Ronald, 1974.

— *The Revelation of Bahá'u'lláh*, vol. 2. Oxford: George Ronald, 1977.

— *The Revelation of Bahá'u'lláh*, vol. 3. Oxford: George Ronald, 1983.

— *The Revelation of Bahá'u'lláh*, vol. 4. Oxford: George Ronald, 1987.

Universal House of Justice. *The Constitution of the Universal House of Justice.* Haifa: Bahá'í World Centre, 1972.

— *Individual Rights and Freedoms in the World Order of Bahá'u'lláh* (29 December 1988). Wilmette IL: Bahá'í Publishing Trust, 1989.

— Letter written on behalf of the Universal House of Justice to an individual, 9 November 1981.

— Letter to the Iranian Believers Throughout the World, March 1997/Bahá 154.

— Letter to the Conference of the Continental Boards of Counsellors, 27 December 2005.

— Letter to the Bahá'ís of the World, Riḍván 154/1997.

— Letter to the Bahá'ís of the World, Riḍván 2008.

— *Messages from the Universal House of Justice 1963–1986: The Third Epoch of the Formative Age*. Wilmette, IL: Bahá'í Publishing Trust, 1996.

— *The Promise of World Peace*. Haifa: Bahá'í World Centre, 1985.

— Second Message to the World Congress, 26 November 1992.

— *Wellspring of Guidance*. Wilmette, IL: Bahá'í Publishing Trust, 1976.

Weil, Henry A. *Closer Than Your Life Vein: An Insight into the Wonders of Spiritual Fulfillment*. New Delhi: Bahá'í Publishing Trust, 1987.

— *Drops from the Ocean*. New Delhi: Bahá'í Publishing Trust, 1987.

— *Wealth without Gold*. Unpublished manuscript.

The Worlds of God: Basic Classifications of Existence as Defined in the Bahá'í Writings. A Compilation prepared by the National Reference Library Committee of the National Spiritual Assembly of the Bahá'ís of the United States, 1965–74.

REFERENCES

The Purpose of This Book

1. Bahá'u'lláh, *Hidden Words*, Arabic no. 2.
2. 'Abdu'l-Bahá, *Promulgation*, p. 465. Emphasis added.
3. The Universal House of Justice, Letter to the Bahá'ís of the World, Riḍván 2008.
4. Bahá'u'lláh, *Hidden Words*, Arabic no. 22.
5. Letter of the Universal House of Justice to the National Spiritual Assembly of Italy, 19 November 1974, in *Messages from the Universal House of Justice 1963–1986*, pp. 282–4. Emphasis added.

Chapter 1: Fighting Evil: 'A Vain Waste of Time and Effort'

1. 'Abdu'l-Bahá, *Promulgation*, p. 433.
2. From a letter written on behalf of Shoghi Effendi, 24 July 1943, in Shoghi Effendi, *High Endeavors*, p. 7.
3. 'Abdu'l-Bahá, *Paris Talks*, pp. 177–8.
4. ibid. pp. 97–8. Emphasis added.
5. Bahá'u'lláh, *Kitáb-i-Íqán*, p. 193. Emphasis added.
6. From a letter written on behalf of Shoghi Effendi an individual, 12 May 1925, in *Lights of Guidance*, p. 88.
7. From a letter written on behalf of the Universal House of Justice to an individual, 23 September 1975, in *Lights of Guidance*, p. 90.
8. 'Abdu'l-Bahá, *Selections*, pp. 229–30.
9. From a letter written on behalf of the Universal House of Justice, 13 August 1980, in *Lights of Guidance*, p. 90.
10. From a letter written on behalf of Shoghi Effendi to the National Spiritual Assembly of the British Isles, 11 February 1925, in *Lights of Guidance*, p. 88.

Chapter 2: The Illness: Blind Imitation

1. Bahá'u'lláh, *Tablets*, p. 157. Emphasis added.
2. Letter of the Universal House of Justice to the National Spiritual

Assembly of Italy, 19 November 1974, in *Messages from the Universal House of Justice 1963–1986*, p. 283.
3. 'Abdu'l-Bahá, *Selections*, p. 247. Emphasis added.
4. 'Abdu'l-Bahá, *Promulgation*, p. 180.
5. *One Common Faith*, para. 1.
6. 'Abdu'l-Bahá, *Promulgation*, p. 41.
7. ibid. p. 161.

Chapter 3: The Remedy: Investigating Reality

1. 'Abdu'l-Bahá, *Promulgation*, p. 169.
2. ibid. p. 180.
3. ibid. p. 344.
4. ibid. p. 433. Emphasis added.
5. 'Abdu'l-Bahá, *Some Answered Questions*, p. 137.
6. 'Abdu'l-Bahá, *Promulgation*, pp. 293–4. Emphasis added.
7. Saiedi, *Gate of the Heart*, pp. 219–20.
8. From a letter written on behalf of Shoghi Effendi to an individual, 5 October 1950, *Compilation*, vol. 2, pp. 22–3.
9. 'Abdu'l-Bahá, *Promulgation*, p. 293.
10. Bahá'u'lláh, *Hidden Words*, Arabic no. 2.
11. Bahá'u'lláh, *Tablets*, p. 157.
12. ibid. Emphasis added.
13. 'Abdu'l-Bahá, *Promulgation*, p. 157. Emphasis added.
14. Bahá'u'lláh, *Tablets*, pp. 166–7. Emphasis added.

Chapter 4: The Two Service Questions

1. 'Abdu'l-Bahá, *Paris Talks*, p. 16. Emphasis added.
2. 'Abdu'l-Bahá, *Traveler's Narrative*, p. 45. Emphasis added.
3. Bahá'u'lláh, *Tablets*, p. 84.
4. Letter of the Universal House of Justice to the Conference of the Continental Boards of Counsellors, 27 December 2005.
5. *'Abdu'l-Bahá in London*, p. 54. Emphasis added.
6. See 'Abdu'l-Bahá, *Selections*, pp. 153–4.
7. Bahá'u'lláh, *Seven Valleys*, p. 5.
8. Taherzadeh, *Revelation of Bahá'u'lláh*, vol. 1, p. 120. Emphasis added.
9. 'Abdu'l-Bahá, *Some Answered Questions*, p. 233.
10. 'Abdu'l-Bahá, *Selections*, p. 158. Emphasis added.
11. 'Abdu'l-Bahá, *Promulgation*, p. 62.
12. Letter of the Universal House of Justice to the Bahá'ís of the World, Riḍván 154/1997.

Chapter 5: General Identity and Individual Identity

1. Bahá'u'lláh, *Tablets*, p. 156.
2. From a letter of the Universal House of Justice to the National Spiritual Assembly of Italy, 19 November 1974, in *Messages from the Universal House of Justice 1963–1986*, pp. 282–4. Emphasis added.
3. Bahá'u'lláh, *Summons*, p. 34.
4. Bahá'u'lláh, *Gleanings*, p. 340.
5. Bahá'u'lláh, *Seven Valleys*, p. 34.
6. Harper, *Universe Within*, p. 79.
7. Bahá'u'lláh, *Gleanings*, pp. 158–9.
8. 'Abdu'l-Bahá, *Some Answered Questions*, p. 230.
9. 'Abdu'l-Bahá, in *Bahá'í World Faith*, p. 329.
10. Bahá'u'lláh, *Kitáb-i-Aqdas*, para. 120.
11. 'Abdu'l-Bahá, *Some Answered Questions*, p. 230.
12. 'Abdu'l-Bahá, quoted in Shoghi Effendi, *World Order*, p. 139.
13. 'Abdu'l-Bahá, *Selections*, p. 76.
14. Bahá'u'lláh, *Prayers and Meditations*, p. 314.
15. Bahá'u'lláh, *Seven Valleys*, p. 5. Emphasis added.
16. From the English translation of a letter of the Universal House of Justice to the Iranian Believers Throughout the World, Bahá 154 BE (March 1997).
17. Taherzadeh, *Covenant of Bahá'u'lláh*, p. 103.
18. Bahá'u'lláh, 'Four Valleys', in *Seven Valleys*, p. 50.
19. Balyuzi, *'Abdu'l-Bahá*, p. 288.
20. 'Abdu'l-Bahá, *Promulgation*, p. 157.
21. Bahá'u'lláh, *Tablets*, p. 162.
22. Bahá'u'lláh, *Tablets*, p. 157.
23. From a letter of the Universal House of Justice to the Bahá'ís of the World, Riḍván 2008.
24. From a Tablet of 'Abdu'l-Bahá, in *Compilation*, vol. 1, no. 578, p. 252.
25. Bahá'u'lláh, *Tablets*, pp. 172–3.
26. 'Abdu'l-Bahá, *Promulgation*, p. 453.
27. 'Abdu'l-Bahá, *Selections*, p. 228. Emphasis added.
28. 'Abdu'l-Bahá, in *Bahá'í Prayers*, p. 69.
29. See Taherzadeh, *Revelation of Bahá'u'lláh*, vol. 2, pp. 282–90.
30. ibid. pp. 286–7.
31. ibid. p. 289.
32. 'Abdu'l-Bahá, *Promulgation*, p. 455.
33. Bahá'u'lláh, 'Four Valleys', in *Seven Valleys*, p. 50.

Chapter 6: 'To What Purpose They Exist'

1. Bahá'u'lláh, *Gleanings*, p. 287.
2. 'Abdu'l-Bahá, *Paris Talks*, p. 177.

3. From a letter of the Universal House of Justice to the National Spiritual Assembly of Italy, 19 November 1974, in *Messages from the Universal House of Justice 1963–1986*, pp. 282–4. Emphasis added.
4. Bahá'u'lláh, *Kitáb-i-Aqdas*, para. 4.
5. Bahá'u'lláh, *Gleanings*, p. 65. Emphasis added.
6. Bahá'u'lláh, *Hidden Words*, Arabic no. 13. Emphasis added.
7. Balyuzi, *'Abdu'l-Bahá*, p. 233.
8. Bahá'u'lláh, *Hidden Words*, Persian no. 69. Emphasis added.
9. Bahá'u'lláh, *Kitáb-i-Aqdas*, para. 70.
10. Marion Jack, quoted in *Bahá'í World*, vol. 12, p. 677.
11. Ruhi Institute, *Teaching the Cause*, p. 89.
12. 'Abdu'l-Bahá, *Paris Talks*, pp. 176–7. Emphasis added.
13. Bahá'u'lláh, *Seven Valleys*, p. 18.
14. 'Abdu'l-Bahá, *Tablets*, vol. 2, p. 430.
15. From a letter of the Universal House of Justice to an individual, 3 January 1982, in *Messages from the Universal House of Justice, 1963–1986*, p. 516. Emphasis added.
16. 'Abdu'l-Bahá, *Selections*, p. 181. Emphasis added.
17. 'Abdu'l-Bahá, in *Bahai Scriptures*, p. 278.
18. Bahá'u'lláh, *Hidden Words*, Arabic no. 48.
19. 'Abdu'l-Bahá, *Promulgation*, p. 469.
20. Bahá'u'lláh, *Prayers and Meditations*, p. 220.
21. 'Abdu'l-Bahá, *Promulgation*, pp. 334–5. Emphasis added.
22. ibid. p. 335.
23. Bahá'u'lláh, *Gleanings*, p. 214.
24. *'Abdu'l-Bahá in London*, p. 121.
25. ibid. p. 120.
26. 'Abdu'l-Bahá, *Paris Talks*, p. 110.
27. ibid. Emphasis added.
28. ibid. p. 18.
29. 'Abdu'l-Bahá, *Some Answered Questions*, p. 240.
30. Bahá'u'lláh, *Seven Valleys*, p. 19.
31. 'Abdu'l-Bahá, in *Bahá'í World Faith*, p. 385.
32. Bahá'u'lláh, *Gleanings*, p. 278. Emphasis added.
33. 'Abdu'l-Bahá, *Bahá'í World Faith*, p. 369. Emphasis added.
34. From a letter of the Universal House of Justice to the National Spiritual Assembly of Italy, 19 November 1974, in *Messages from the Universal House of Justice 1963–1986*, pp. 282–4. Emphasis added.
35. See www.nicholasgreen.org

Chapter 7: The Spirit of Faith

1. 'Abdu'l-Bahá, *Some Answered Questions*, pp. 144–5. Emphasis added.
2. ibid. p. 144.

3. 'Abdu'l-Bahá, in *Bahá'í World Faith*, p. 371. Emphasis added.
4. 'Abdu'l-Bahá, *Some Answered Questions*, p. 209.
5. ibid. p. 208. Emphasis added.
6. 'Abdu'l-Bahá, in *Bahá'í World Faith*, pp. 370–1. Emphasis added.
7. 'Abdu'l-Bahá, *Some Answered Questions*, pp. 241–2.
8. Bahá'u'lláh, *Hidden Words*, Arabic no. 59.
9. Letter of the Universal House of Justice to the Conference of the Continental Boards of Counsellors, 27 December 2005.
10. Bahá'u'lláh, *Gleanings*, pp. 65–8.
11. See, for example, Taherzadeh, *Revelation of Bahá'u'lláh*, vol. 1, pp. 73–5.
12. Taherzadeh, *Revelation of Bahá'u'lláh*, vol. 1, p. 73.
13. ibid. p. 74.
14. Bahá'u'lláh, *Gleanings*, p. 327.

Chapter 8: Using the Faculty of Inner Vision

1. 'Abdu'l-Bahá, *Promulgation*, p. 90. Emphasis added.
2. ibid.
3. 'Abdu'l-Bahá, *Paris Talks*, p. 86. Emphasis added.
4. Bahá'u'lláh, *Gleanings*, pp. 267–8.
5. 'Abdu'l-Bahá, in *'Abdu'l-Bahá in London*, p. 46.
6. 'Abdu'l-Bahá, *Some Answered Questions*, p. 283.
7. 'Abdu'l-Bahá, in *Bahá'í World Faith*, p. 369. Emphasis added.
8. 'Abdu'l-Bahá, *Some Answered Questions*, p. 218. Emphasis added.
9. 'Abdu'l-Bahá, *Secret of Divine Civilization*, p. 21.
10. 'Abdu'l-Bahá, *Paris Talks*, p. 174.
11. ibid. p. 175.
12. Bahá'u'lláh, *Hidden Words*, Persian no. 12.
13. 'Abdu'l-Bahá, *Paris Talks*, pp. 173–6.
14. ibid. p. 174.
15. ibid. Emphasis added.
16. ibid. p. 175.
17. Bahá'u'lláh, *Prayers and Meditations*, p. 249.
18. Bahá'u'lláh, *Hidden Words*, Arabic no. 6. Emphasis added.
19. Saiedi, *Gate of the Heart*, p. 164.
20. 'Abdu'l-Bahá, in *Bahá'í World Faith*, p. 369.
21. 'Abdu'l-Bahá, *Some Answered Questions*, p. 218. Emphasis added.
22. A ḥadíth quoted by Bahá'u'lláh in 'Four Valleys' in *Seven Valleys*, p. 54.
23. 'Abdu'l-Bahá, *Paris Talks*, p. 176.
24. Bahá'u'lláh, *Seven Valleys*, p. 5. Emphasis added.
25. Bahá'u'lláh, *Kitáb-i-Íqán*, p. 192. Emphasis added.
26. 'Abdu'l-Bahá, *Promulgation*, p. 90.
27. Bahá'u'lláh, *Kitáb-i-Íqán*, p. 68.

Chapter 9: Servant to Truth

1. 'Abdu'l-Bahá, *Promulgation*, p. 291.
2. 'Abdu'l-Bahá, *Some Answered Questions*, pp. 208–9. Emphasis added.
3. 'Abdu'l-Bahá, *Selections*, p. 228.
4. ibid.
5. Bahá'u'lláh, *Hidden Words*, Persian no. 19.
6. Taherzadeh, *Covenant of Bahá'u'lláh*, p. 388.
7. From a letter of the Universal House of Justice, 27 May 1966, in Universal House of Justice, *Wellspring of Guidance*, p. 84.
8. Taherzadeh, *Revelation of Bahá'u'lláh*, vol. 1, pp. 80–1.
9. Bahá'u'lláh, in *Compilation*, vol. 1, p. 93.
10. Shoghi Effendi, *Bahá'í Administration*, p. 22.
11. Gleaned from quotations in 'Consultation', *Compilation*, vol. 1, pp. 93–110.
12. 'Abdu'l-Bahá, *Selections*, p. 87. Emphasis added.
13. 'Abdu'l-Bahá, *Paris Talks*, p. 89.
14. 'Abdu'l-Bahá, *Some Answered Questions*, p. 73.
15. *'Abdu'l-Bahá in London*, p. 46.
16. 'Abdu'l-Bahá, *Some Answered Questions*, p. 283.
17. ibid. p. 233.
18. ibid. p. 232.
19. ibid.
20. Hatcher, *Purpose of Physical Reality*, pp. 145, 144.
21. Laura Clifford Barney, quoted in 'Abdu'l-Bahá, *Some Answered Questions*, p. 239; see also p. 208. Emphasis added.
22. 'Abdu'l-Bahá, in *Bahá'í World Faith*, pp. 370–1. Emphasis added.
23. 'Abdu'l-Bahá, *Some Answered Questions*, p. 240. Emphasis added.

Chapter 10: Coming Home to Our Spiritual Nature

1. The Universal House of Justice, Second Message to World Congress, 26 November 1992.
2. Bahá'u'lláh, *Prayers and Meditations*, p. 288.
3. 'Abdu'l-Bahá, *Promulgation*, p. 465.
4. 'Abdu'l-Bahá, *Paris Talks*, pp. 97–8.
5. Letter of the Universal House of Justice to the National Spiritual Assembly of Italy, 19 November 1974, in *Messages from the Universal House of Justice 1963–1986*, pp. 282–4.
6. 'Abdu'l-Bahá, *Paris Talks*, p. 97.
7. 'Abdu'l-Bahá, *Foundations of World Unity*, p. 110.
8. ibid. p. 51.
9. From a letter written on behalf of Shoghi Effendi to Alfred Lunt, 1936, in *Lights of Guidance*, p. 208. Emphasis added.
10. 'Abdu'l-Bahá, *Promulgation*, pp. 294–5.

11. 'Abdu'l-Bahá, *Some Answered Questions*, p. 144. Emphasis added.
12. 'Abdu'l-Bahá, *Promulgation*, p. 230.
13. 'Abdu'l-Bahá, *Some Answered Questions*, p. 264.
14. 'Abdu'l-Bahá, *Paris Talks*, p. 177.
15. 'Abdu'l-Bahá, *Some Answered Questions*, ch. 74, pp. 262–4.
16. 'Abdu'l-Bahá, *Paris Talks*, p. 51. Emphasis added.
17. Hatcher, *Close Connections*, p. 270. Emphasis added.
18. 'Abdu'l-Bahá, *Some Answered Questions*, p. 143. Emphasis added.
19. 'Abdu'l-Bahá, *Promulgation*, p. 357.
20. LeDoux, *Emotional Brain*, p. 165.
21. 'Abdu'l-Bahá, *Selections*, p. 247.
22. 'Abdu'l-Bahá, in *Bahá'í World Faith*, p. 370.
23. ibid. p. 317.
24. 'Abdu'l-Bahá, *Some Answered Questions*, p. 208. Emphasis added.
25. 'Abdu'l-Bahá, *Promulgation*, p. 32.
26. ibid. p. 33.
27. 'Abdu'l-Bahá, in *Bahá'í World Faith*, p. 260.
28. 'Abdu'l-Bahá, *Paris Talks*, p. 51.
29. Hatcher, *Love, Power and Justice*, p. 88.
30. Bahá'u'lláh, *Seven Valleys*, pp. 17–18.
31. Bahá'u'lláh, *Hidden Words*, Arabic no. 59.
32. Bahá'u'lláh, *Tablets*, p. 158. Emphasis added.
33. Bahá'u'lláh, *Seven Valleys*, p. 5.
34. ibid. p. 35. Emphasis added.
35. Saiedi, *Gate of the Heart*, p. 50.
36. ibid. p. 14.
37. Harper, *Universe Within*, p. 76.

Appendix 2: Selected Quotations about Our Created Purposes

1. Bahá'u'lláh, *Kitáb-i-Aqdas*, p. 100.
2. Bahá'u'lláh, *Gleanings*, pp. 77–8.
3. Bahá'u'lláh, *Epistle to the Son of the Wolf*, p. 3.
4. 'Abdu'l-Bahá, quoted in Bahá'u'lláh, *Kitáb-i-Aqdas*, Notes, p. 176.
5. Bahá'u'lláh, *Epistle to the Son of the Wolf*, p. 26.
6. Bahá'u'lláh, 'Fire Tablet', in *Bahá'í Prayers*, p. 317.
7. The Greatest Holy Leaf, in *Bahíyyih Khánum*, pp. 97–8.
8. Bahá'u'lláh, *Epistle to the Son of the Wolf*, p. 37.
9. Bahá'u'lláh, *Gleanings*, p. 215.
10. Bahá'u'lláh, *Tablets*, p. 138.
11. Bahá'u'lláh, *Summons*, para. 3.26.
12. 'Abdu'l-Bahá, *Foundations of World Unity*, p. 42.
13. 'Abdu'l-Bahá, *Paris Talks*, p. 177.
14. ibid. p. 113.

15. 'Abdu'l-Bahá, *Promulgation*, p. 469.
16. ibid. p. 353.
17. 'Abdu'l-Bahá, in *Abdu'l-Bahá in London*, p. 29.
18. 'Abdu'l-Bahá, *Promulgation*, p. 32.
19. Shoghi Effendi, *Messages to America*, pp. 27–8.
20. From a letter written on behalf of Shoghi Effendi to the Louhelen School Youth Session, 25 August 1944, in *Compilation*, vol. 2, no. 1300.

Appendix 3: References for Statements about Blind Imitation

1. 'Abdu'l-Bahá, *Promulgation*, p. 39.
2. ibid. p. 41.
3. ibid.
4. ibid. pp. 153, 158.
5. ibid. p. 161.
6. ibid.
7. ibid.
8. ibid.
9. ibid.
10. ibid.
11. ibid.
12. ibid. p. 180.
13. ibid.
14. ibid. p. 291.
15. ibid. p. 339.
16. 'Abdu'l-Bahá, *Selections*, p. 247.
17. ibid. p. 248.
18. ibid. p. 253.
19. 'Abdu'l-Bahá, *Promulgation*, p. 441.
20. ibid. p. 291.
21. ibid. p. 274.
22. ibid. p. 294.
23. ibid. p. 153.
24. ibid. p. 161.
25. ibid. p. 179.
26. ibid. p. 161.
27. ibid. p. 179.
28. ibid. p. 443.
29. ibid. p. 42.
30. ibid. p. 443.
31. ibid. p. 41.
32. ibid. p. 198.
33. ibid. pp. 221–2.

34. ibid. p. 39.
35. 'Abdu'l-Bahá, *Selections*, p. 247.
36. ibid. p. 439.
37. 'Abdu'l-Bahá, *Promulgation*, p. 86.
38. ibid. p. 39.
39. 'Abdu'l-Bahá, *Secret of Divine Civilization*, p. 104.
40. 'Abdu'l-Bahá, *Promulgation*, p. 198.
41. ibid.
42. ibid. p. 364.
43. From a letter of Shoghi Effendi to the Bahá'ís of the East, 19 December 1923, in *Compilation*, vol. 2, no. 1268.

Appendix 4: The Guidance of Souls

1. The Báb, *Selections*, p. 77.
2. The Universal House of Justice, 19 November 1974. Emphasis added.
3. 'Abdu'l-Bahá, *Selections*, p. 265.
4. ibid. p. 76.
5. Bahá'u'lláh, *Hidden Words*, Persian no. 12.
6. Bahá'u'lláh, *Epistle to the Son of the Wolf*, p. 111.

Appendix 5: The Guiding Light of the Fear of God

1. 'Abdu'l-Bahá, *Promulgation*, p. 89.
2. Bahá'u'lláh, 'Four Valleys', *Seven Valleys*, p. 58.
3. *'Abdu'l-Bahá in London*, p. 46.
4. 'Abdu'l-Bahá, *Some Answered Questions*, p. 283.
5. ibid. p. 230.
6. Bahá'u'lláh, *Seven Valleys*, p. 11. Emphasis added.
7. Bahá'u'lláh, *Epistle to the Son of the Wolf*, p. 27. Emphasis added.
8. Bahá'u'lláh, *Kitáb-i-Aqdas*, para. 120. Emphasis added.
9. Quoted by Bahá'u'lláh in 'Four Valleys', in *Seven Valleys*, p. 58.
10. 'Abdu'l-Bahá, *Divine Philosophy*, pp. 135–7.
11. ibid. p. 137.
12. See 'Abdu'l-Bahá, *Some Answered Questions*, p. 6.
13. Quoted by Bahá'u'lláh, in 'Four Valleys', in *Seven Valleys*, p. 58.
14. Bahá'u'lláh, *Kitáb-i-Aqdas*, para. 120.
15. 'Abdu'l-Bahá, *Selections*, p. 181. Emphasis added.
16. Bahá'u'lláh, *Seven Valleys*, p. 11.
17. Bahá'u'lláh, *Gleanings*, p. 268.
18. Bahá'u'lláh, *Hidden Words*, Arabic no. 3.
19. ibid. Persian no. 19.